"America began as a church
being uprooted. Wisdom dic
we must replant the churche   ...p.u....e. s,
Jim Harrell's masterpiece is a must read. "

- Rev. Dr. William Boylan, Senior Pastor Byfield Parish Church,
Georgetown, MA

"Dr. Jim Harrell passionately believes God can heal and restore lost
churches. Church Replanter is a mighty call to raise an army of God's
people to bring new life to struggling churches. I highly recommend
Dr. Harrell's book as a great resource to those interested in partaking
in this important outreach or to churches praying for God to breathe
in them new life."

- Rev. Dr. John Lloyd, Senior Pastor Christ Community
Church, East Taunton, MA

"Author Jim Harrell introduces us to the term "replanting." The word
may be new but the concept is as old as the seven churches in
Revelation. We are reminded that Jesus Christ has been replanting
and renewing His church ever since its earliest days. Dr. Harrell helps
us understand the process of how God uses patient, faithful pastors
to revitalize once thriving but now declining historic churches. This
book is essential reading for anyone called to the challenging but
fulfilling work of replanting."

—Rev. Dr. Jack L Daniel, Semi-retired Replanter

CHURCH REPLANTER

Learning from Nehemiah's example of leading change when things are really broken.

DR. JIM HARRELL

Overseed PRESS

Church Replanter
Published by Overseed Press
Division of William & James Publishing
36 W Ox Pasture Ln
Rowley, MA 01969 U.S.A

The website references recommended throughout this book are offered as a resource to you. These websites are not intended in any way to be or imply an endorsement on the part of William & James Publishing, nor do we vouch for their content.

ISBN 978-1-940151-00-7

Editor: Aileen Richards
Cover Design: Amy Allaire

Printed in the United States of America
First Edition 2015

FOREWORD

When Richard Baxter, at the age of twenty-six, assumed his new pastoral duties at St. Mary and All Saints' Church in the heart of England, he knew that he would be facing some formidable challenges. Kidderminster's spacious sanctuary, a building that dominated the village of middle-class trades people, was seldom visited by more than a handful of worshippers and the parishioners themselves were better known for their divisiveness, immorality and opposition to the Gospel than they were for their Christian piety. "If I were asked what, in the year 1646, was one of the most unpromising towns in England to which a young man could be sent, who was starting his career as a preacher and pastor," wrote John Brown, "I should feel inclined at once to point to the town of Kidderminster in Worcestershire." Indeed, one would hardly have blamed the gifted young preacher had he decided to turn down such a daunting challenge in favor of more promising opportunities elsewhere.

Rather than run from the challenge, however, Baxter chose to embrace it and the results of that decision were absolutely astounding. Over the course of his remarkable ministry in Kidderminster, the spiritual life of that entire community was quite literally transformed. Through faithful preaching of the Word, fervent prayer, godly leadership, compassionate discipline, and systematic discipleship, an historic but troubled congregation -- by God's grace -- was given the gift of new life and hope.

Such spiritual transformations are as urgently needed today as they were in seventeenth-century England. For sprinkled across the New England landscape -- and indeed around the globe -- are

5

literally hundreds of churches whose pews are largely empty, whose budgets are nearly depleted and whose spiritual vitality has been gradually drained despite their rich and vibrant histories. They too, by God's grace, could enjoy the kind of spiritual rebirth and renewal that St. Mary and All Saints' experienced during the seventeenth century. This is precisely the vision that God has laid on the heart of my good friend, Dr. Jim Harrell -- a vision that has spawned Overseed Ministries and that has given birth to the valuable new resource that you now hold in your hands.

Indeed, God seems in our day to be raising-up a whole new generation of Christian leaders who are eager to embrace the same kind of challenge that inspired Richard Baxter many years ago. If that is becoming your vision, then let me encourage you to read and re-read *Church Replanter: Learning from Nehemiah's Example of Leading Change when Things are really Broken.* It will instruct, inspire and encourage you as you join the growing band of "replanters" that God is using to bring new life and spiritual vitality to His beloved church.

Dr. Garth M. Rosell, Professor of Church History
Gordon-Conwell Theological Seminary

For Sharon my wife and my children Katie, Amy and John. My family has taught me so much about love, shepherding and friendship. May God extend their impact in His Kingdom!

I wish to thank Dr. Bill Boylan for his example of steadfastly loving his congregation and untold number of hours he has spent with me discussing this vision and sharing with me his experiences of leading renewal at Byfield Parish Church in Georgetown, MA.

CONTENTS

Foreword 5

Introduction... 11

1. Replanting A Broken Church 25

2. Being Called of God 37

3. Responding to God's Call....................................... 49

4. Beginning the Change Process 67

5. Expect Pushback Against Change 81

6. Lasting Change Requires Infrastructure & Intentionality... 107

7. Revitalization is an Ongoing Process 143

Conclusion 155

Appendix A – Replanter Profile 163

Appendix B – Stages of Decline 165

Why Overseed 171

INTRODUCTION

Potential Replanter: So when a church is broken and dwindles down to a small congregation, is there any hope of them surviving long term?

God: *"Shout for joy, O barren one, you who have borne no child; break forth into joyful shouting and cry aloud, you who have not travailed; for the sons of the desolate one will be more numerous than the sons of the married woman," says the LORD. "Enlarge the place of your tent; stretch out the curtains of your dwellings, spare not; lengthen your cords and strengthen your pegs. "For you will spread abroad to the right and to the left. And your descendants will possess nations and will resettle the desolate cities. (Isaiah 54:1–3)*

INTRODUCTION

In the fall 1999, I attended a historic New England church for the first time.[1] It was founded in 1603. The church had been renewed in early 1970's. When the replant pastor arrived, there were 11 people and now over 200 regular attenders worship at the church each Sunday. The replanter, a young evangelical man from the local seminary, had been hired, mostly because they couldn't get anyone else qualified to come to be their pastor. Difficult would be an understatement to describe the early years of his pastorate. Miraculous would be an accurate statement to describe what God did to replant this church.

In 1999, I was attending Gordon Conwell Theological Seminary on my way to plant a church with the Baptist General Church (now Converge). I had been through their church planter torture test (known as an assessment center) and had been approved as a church replanter. My wife and I were looking forward to church planting in the near future.

Yet, each Sunday as I attended this historic church, while I was at seminary, there were these questions swirling around in my head. Why pastor a church like that? Why stay at this kind of church for 40 plus years? Why waste your life doing that when you could be a part of a large happening church or plant one? As the year went on, it was obvious this pastor had stayed at this church because of vision and God's calling. However, it didn't make sense to me and I wanted to understand it.

---

[1] My spiritual roots though are in the historic church. My mother attended an Evangelical Reformed church when she was growing up. The Evangelical Reformed church merged with the Congregational churches to form the UCC in the last 1950s.

I finished seminary but God made it clear that He wasn't calling me into church planting. So my wife and I served at this historic church by restarting/revitalizing the youth group while we waited for God to reveal His will for us. About six years after we had started attending the church, I had the privilege of interviewing the pastor and his wife. I listened to the stories of those early years, his calling to this church, the pain of those initial years, the amazing love extended to difficult people, of how God brought folks to the church and to Himself. I listened to him and his wife talk about how God has used them to also help initiate renewal in other historic New England churches.

The next week I was sleeping on the floor of a Baptist church with the youth group in downtown Dorchester, an older historic neighborhood of Boston. We had done to Boston to serve with the Boston Project[2] for a few days over spring break. It was 5:30 in the morning and I went outside in search of coffee. I was walking down the middle of the street (not much traffic at 5:30am) and as I came around the corner, I saw a large New England historic church trying to raise money to fix the roof (pretty good sign of declining numbers).

I stood in the middle of the street thinking and praying. If I was going to plant a church in Dorchester where would I do it? There is no land for sale in Dorchester. I could use a store front, a school, or a movie theater and there is nothing wrong with those

---

[2]The Boston Project engages neighbors and volunteers to build and nurture strong communities, characterized by God's shalom. The Boston Project Ministries (TBPM) was originally formed in 1995 by a group of Gordon College students to mobilize teenage volunteers in faith-based service throughout Boston. To learn more see their website at http://www.tbpm.org.

options. But the thought occurred to me, why not plant a churches in existing churches that are dying?

God and I had a conversation for about 30 minutes about how that might work. It has its difficulties and its positive components. I thought about my own church planting experiences, about the pastor's story of renewing his church, with hundreds of people coming to Christ. The Byfield Parish church had once again became a local religious lighthouse to the surrounding community and was used by God to influence numerous other churches on the North Shore of Boston, who also began revitalizing.

I began strategizing how this might work. It became increasingly clear that replanting could be a very fruitful evangelistic strategy for New England. As we talked, I told God, "I'm in. God, You will need to do what you always need to do – change people's hearts – but I'm in."

I struggled with how to explain this vision and started to use the term "replanting." I googled the term and couldn't find any references to term replanting in the any context related to churches. I found terms like restart, but restart and the terms related to it, referred more to concept of shutting down a dying church and then starting it back up some months later with different branding. The term "replant" seemed better fitted to describing what God was laying on my heart.[3]

It soon became obvious that in independent New England, a separate organization was needed to help facilitate this vision of

---

[3] Since 2007, the word has popped up in numerous places to describe this process of church renewal. When God is up to something He often calls multiple people to the same idea in different locations.

replanting declining New England churches, rather than trying to center that vision in a one local church. Thus, in the summer of 2008, Overseed was formed. Overseed's vision is to replant/revitalize historic New England churches in order to awaken communities to Christ by:

- Recruiting and coaching historic New England church leaders in intentional renewal strategies
- Recruiting and coaching pastors committed to the gospel to serve in historic New England churches
- Partnering with larger regional "Overseed HUB" churches who provide pulpit supply, coaching and other resources to help declining churches in surrounding communities

The more I have studied church replanting, the more I am convinced that this is a key evangelistic strategy for New England.

However, unlike church planting, church *replanting* starts from a historic trajectory and with an existing congregation. Replanting requires change and leading change is always problematic, primarily because people do not want to change. As one friend told me, "People who say they want to change, are lying." While that may be extreme, the truth is that most people do not welcome change.

When someone is in difficulty, especially if it is self-induced through bad habits, outsiders often assume that the person wants to change but for various reasons is unable. Those in addiction recovery ministries are quick to point out a different truth exits; these people don't want to change and until they do, there is little chance of change happening.

When a broken person truly does decide to change, they typically need leadership, guidance and accountability. They need someone to help point the way forward, to give them instructions on life skills and to hold them accountable for making forward progress. But it all must begin with that person's realization that their life is broken. The person must agree that a change is needed and want to change.

This is also true of churches, or more accurately, true of the people who make up a particular church. A broken church[4] must want to change. Yes, a broken church that has chosen to change will need leadership, guidance, and accountability. Unfortunately, just like broken people, broken churches often don't know they are broken, even if their brokenness is obvious to those around them.[5]

When is a church broken? At what point does a congregation come to the conclusion that they are behaving like a dysfunctional family? When does a church's leadership board face the reality that they are not doing a good job leading their church?

The unfortunate truth is that rarely do those in such a church realize how badly the church is broken until there has been serious decline. They may have a vague sense that things could be better, that a few more givers would be helpful, that in days gone by the church was thriving, but for them to embrace the reality that their church is broken is a whole other thing. Understandably, no one

---

[4] The author wrestled with using the term broken, as there is no intent to be pejorative. The term is only being used to describe the reality of the church's situation from Christ's perspective.

[5] Churches get ingrown and the focus becomes "us" and what do "we" want. Often what "we" want is for things to stay the same. Thom Rainer has a great blog entry describing an inward focused church.
http://thomrainer.com/2012/05/02/the_inwardly_obsessed_church_10_warning_signs/

wants to see their church as broken but it is better to humbly acknowledge the situation and face reality. Otherwise, a broken church stays broken.

In a broken church, the cycle of decline, conflict and passive-aggressive behavior continues unabated as the church cycles through various pastors. Search committees keep hiring the same kind of co-dependent pastor, who facilitates their unhelpful[6] approach to church, leadership, and relationships. It is sort of like the girl from a dysfunctional family who goes to a party, walks by all the healthy boys and saddles up to a dysfunctional guy because he looks and feels normal to her.

This cycle of brokenness is not easily altered. Corporate change, like Individual change, is hard. Sanctifying individuals and churches takes the power of God. A broken church needs the Holy Spirit to lead and empower God's people to embrace and live out His word, so they can be the church.

The primary means that the Holy Spirit uses to facilitate this change is God's word. Paul tells us that the gospel is the power of God for salvation to everyone who believes.[7] The Holy Spirit changes people when God's revelation of Himself in scripture is met with faith. It is often not quick or flashy, but the Holy Spirit causes steady healing and growth to take place.

The foundation for leading change in a broken church is not better methods, updated technology, or better people. Paul explains in 1 Corinthians that the central foundation for leading change is the gospel:

_____

[6] Typically because the approach is unbiblical.
[7] Romans 1:16.

"For the word of the cross is folly to those who are perishing, but to us who are being saved it is the power of God. For it is written, I will destroy the wisdom of the wise, and the discernment of the discerning I will thwart." Where is the one who is wise? Where is the scribe? Where is the debater of this age? Has not God made foolish the wisdom of the world? For since, in the wisdom of God, the world did not know God through wisdom, it pleased God through the folly of what we preach to save those who believe. For Jews demand signs and Greeks seek wisdom, but we preach Christ crucified, a stumbling block to Jews and folly to Gentiles, but to those who are called, both Jews and Greeks, Christ the power of God and the wisdom of God.[8]

Renewing God's church has to begin with God's word. This means that it must begin from the pulpit. If people in the church are to become the people God intended them to be, then they need to hear, to understand, and to believe God's word, Sunday after Sunday. There is no other pathway to health.

Unfortunately, many historic churches have become theologically compromised.[9] Preachers, for various historical and personal reasons, have moved away from the preaching of the historic gospel from the scriptures, denying the supernatural, redefining sin and holiness. Over time, this unbiblical preaching has caused the church to become spiritually anemic, to slip into

---

[8] 1 Corinthians 1:18–24. [ESV].

[9] Again, there is no desire to be disparaging to those who may think otherwise. The author comes from a historical protestant exegetical framework and believes the deviation from that framework is the key significant cause of decline in historic churches.

mediocrity, and has produced a generation of church leaders who border on being gospel illiterate.

The result is a broken church. Ezekiel 22:23-31 describes what such a broken community will eventually look like. It is one where the political and spiritual leaders are living for their own advancement, and the people are following the leader's example. Selfishness and personal preference drive decision making rather than God's word and love for others. Holiness is redefined to make sin acceptable, while the concerns and commands of God are rendered irrelevant.

God's strategy for renewing a broken community among His people in the Old Testament was to look for someone to stand in the gap. Someone to be intentional about restoring the people to God by praying for them and teaching them God's word. The same is true of a broken church. God's typical strategy is to call a replanter to that church to stand in the gap, to pray for the people, and to preach and teach His word as a primary means of restoring the people to God.

Once a church is broken and is in serious decline, often the only way forward is to hire a pastor who will pray for them, once again preach the historic gospel, and lovingly lead the church. This however raises two challenges to a theologically compromised, declining historic church.

First, there is a pastor shortage problem. Many seminary students who are trained to preach the historic gospel are not considering a renewal ministry. Our culture promotes "new" not "renew." Thus many seminary students are considering church planting not replanting. They don't realize the tremendous evangelistic opportunity that church replanting provides.

Secondly, there is a congregational problem. Many of these theologically compromised, declining churches don't know what a joy it is to feed on the historic gospel from the scriptures each week. They have never experienced how a holy God saves us through the grace and truth that are found in Jesus Christ and his atoning death on the cross. Thus they don't know what kind of pastor to look for when there is a pastoral turnover.

The way forward requires a twofold strategy of recruiting bible preaching pastors to seek out replanting opportunities and to help search committees break the pattern of hiring the wrong kind of pastor. [10]

This book is focused on the first problem, the need for pastors who preach the historic gospel in replant situations and manage the renewal process with God given wisdom. This book is about being a pastor who, by God's grace, leads a broken church to health.

The pathway to health often appears clear in the big picture and yet the details and timing are quite fuzzy. There is no magic formula that a pastor can apply to heal the church. Nor can one clone churches. What works in one church may or may not be helpful in another church.

---

[10] The ministry of Overseed embraces this two strategies in order to replant/revitalize historic churches. They engage historic churches in order to help them be intentional about renewal and by recruiting and coaching evangelical pastors to serve in these historic churches. Additional detail on Overseed can be found at the end of the book.

The nuances of the way forward for a particular church is known only by God. Each church resides in a particular location, with particular resources, with a particular history, and with a particular set of people, who have a particular set of gifts and talents. The pastor and the congregation need to seek out God, asking Him what His will is for that particular church.

The good news is that God has shown over and over again in scripture that He delights to renew His people when they seek Him and His will. The road is often not quick or easy but the call to renewal is at its core, a call for the replanter to take up his/her cross and follow Jesus.

The nuances of renewal can also look different in various churches, but fortunately there is also a commonality to the principles of renewal. Despite the fuzziness of a particular local implementation, there are some overarching principles related to timing, leadership, and opposition. As part of the preparation for replanting, the replant pastor needs to understand what God has revealed in scripture about the dynamics involved in renewal, to get a mental picture of what the process looks likes, and to understand how renewal has played out in other local church situations.

The most complete picture we have of renewal happening in one particular community is in the Old Testament book of Nehemiah. This Old Testament book lays out for us the details of both the civic and spiritual renewal of Jerusalem under Nehemiah's leadership.[11] The end result of Nehemiah's tenure, by God's grace,

---

[11] When studying the story of Nehemiah one must remember that this is about both civic and spiritual renewal. Jerusalem was not a church. However, there are many dynamics of the story that overlap with church renewal. One must first understand Nehemiah's context before extrapolating from his situation into a church renewal situation.

was the healing of a broken community who was once again healthy, vibrant and flourishing.

Nehemiah was the man who God called to lead the community of Jerusalem and surrounding towns through the difficulties of renewal. Nehemiah had to navigate through the various complexities of his situation. He lived in the palace, the civic center of the kingdom, with its own particular customs and ways of doing life. Jerusalem was a place far away with both similar and different customs and ideas about life. Nehemiah was Jewish so there was some cultural overlap but there was also bound to be serious disconnect between the cultures of each location. Nehemiah had to begin with the people and situation into which he was called. He had to have to overcome the obstacles as they presented themselves.

In the pages that follow, we are going to walk with Nehemiah as he leads Jerusalem from brokenness to health. It was difficult but God used him to be the catalyst for godly change. Nehemiah lives out the dynamics of replanting, accomplishing what most would have described as nearly impossible, the renewal of Jerusalem.

It is my prayer that God might use you to be a similar catalyst for godly change in the place where He has called you. It is a tremendous blessing and calling to replant/revitalize a church.

CHAPTER 1

REPLANTING A BROKEN CHURCH

Author   Why would anyone replant a historic, theologically compromised, declining New England Church? Sounds impossible and like a complete waste of time.

God   That sounds similar to something I have heard somewhere before….

          The word of the LORD came to Jonah the son of Amittai saying, "Arise, go to Nineveh the great city and cry against it, for their wickedness has come up before Me." But Jonah rose up to flee to Tarshish from the presence of the LORD. So he went down to Joppa, found a ship which was going to Tarshish, paid the fare and went down into it to go with them to Tarshish from the presence of the LORD. [12]

---

[12] Jonah 1:1–3.

1 - REPLANTING A BROKEN CHURCH

The first question in many people's minds before "the how" of renewing a theologically compromised, declining historic church is "the why?" Why spend the time and effort to replant a broken church? Why not just let it die and start over. Especially in a technology advanced culture, which considers a piece of hardware that is 3 years old as ancient and useless. Why mess with a 300 year old church with only a handful of elderly people left in it?

There are good biblical and missional answer to that question.

First, Jesus loves His bride. He doesn't only love the large gatherings, but He is also present where two or three are gathered together in His name. Age, style, and effectiveness is not the criteria by which Jesus decides whether to show up at a church but rather it is a gathering of people with a faith in Christ. This is true regardless of how spiritually immature and broken the people and organizational structures may be.

Jesus desires for His sheep to be watched over. He calls men and women to be shepherds over His flock. Christ desires his people to be taken care of, to be discipled, and to be banded together as a missional family in order to bring His message of love and forgiveness to their local community and to the world. It is not an inferior calling to lead any of Christ's churches.

Secondly, replanting churches also has a strategic missional answer. Planting churches in smaller towns and communities is typically harder than replanting churches, which has been the experience of many failed church plants in New England.

A new pastor coming in to plant a church in such a town, who is "from away"[13] has no trust and has many barriers in the way of building real relationships. Especially, if the pastor goes to a town where people trace their roots back to pre-revolutionary war generations. Many of the relationships in such a town go back generations and a new comer is viewed with serious suspicion and given little trust. Yet, when if that same new person comes to pastor an established church with historic ties to the community, he or she is supposed to be there. There are still barriers to building new relationships but the bar is much lower.

Ministering to an established church allows one to reach out to the community from the inside, often from the center of town. In addition, there is a church building and other resources to work with. Plus, even small churches have a basic infrastructure in place, such as someone to pay the bills, which allows a new pastor to spend less time on administration and more time focused on ministering.[14]

There are good biblical and missional reasons to replant a church but one must undertake a replant with their eyes open. Leading a church replanting effort is no easy task. It requires an abundance of love, patience, and wisdom combined with a long-term strategy. Replanting requires a clear call of God in order to persevere, because laying down the foundations of change can take significant time and energy.

---

[13] "From away" is a typical Maine expression for someone who is not from this town.

[14] Note that existing buildings can be a blessing but they can also make a potential church replant more difficult. Older churches may need extensive repair or the existing structures may not have the design allowing the types of ministry often desired in the 21st century. Thus, they may require extensive reconstruction often at a significant cost. Also, some older church buildings have been designated as historic sites, which severely limits how the building can be changed, and dictates how the construction must take place, usually increasing the cost.

As was mentioned above, most people don't like to change regardless of what they might indicate. People don't realize how strongly they are holding onto their cultural preferences until someone attempts to change them. Thus, the same people who agree to the general concept of change in order to grow the church are the ones often found fighting specific changes to the surprise of the new pastor.

These preferences often show up eventually in either one of two areas: values or procedures. People assume the replant pastor values what they do rather than asking you and thus they are surprised and irritated when they discover his/her values are different. Also, people get very used to doing things a certain way; it is comfortable to them and takes little thought or effort. If you change that procedure than you adding work to their life, which is often unappreciated.

In addition, rebuilding the base foundation is only the first phase of many phases. A successful church replant requires continued development, strengthening, and equipping of the church community. There are always forces at work attempting to reverse any revitalization efforts. Sometimes those efforts are visible, often those efforts are happening below the surface and take the replanter by surprise. The replanter needs to be intentional about continuing to move the church forward. Otherwise, the revitalization work won't have sustaining power, nor the ability to move out into the community with the gospel.

The difficulty of a church replant is compounded for an evangelical choosing to serve in a historic church, because that church culture is often very different from what most evangelicals have experienced. An evangelical pastor taking a pastorate in a historic church is similar to an American setting foot in England as a missionary. Nothing is as it seems because the two cultures, while resembling each other, are not the same. I regularly talk with evangelical pastors who are very confused by the behavior and thinking of an historic congregation they are trying to serve, even after several years of ministry.

In order to be an effective missionary, one must work at studying the different cultural values and priorities of the country where he/she will be ministering in order to understand how to make necessary personal adjustments required to be able to communicate to those in that country. The same is true for an evangelical moving into a historic denomination. The replanter needs to take the time to understand why people believe what they believe, and act the way they do. It is only then that the replanter can make the required personal adjustments in order to love and communicate to those in the church.

Some of the cultural differences are actually better than what the replanter has previously experienced. For example, a historic church often has a deeply embedded mentality of engaging in social justice issues, which many evangelical churches would do well to emulate. Many leaders in historic churches have learned how to disagree amicably with other leaders despite strong disagreements, a skillset that evangelicals could learn from.

Some of the culture differences are neutral. They are simply the preferences of that church community. They may not be the replanter's personal preference but they are not wrong, just different. A replanter needs to understand these local preferences before any attempt is made to alter them. Otherwise the replanter will justly be open to the charge of simply imposing his/her will upon the congregation over against their will.

And some of the cultural differences are bad. They are sinful and destructive. These negative cultural influences result in dysfunctional behavior patterns. The replanter is going to need to address these cultural belief systems, values and priorities with grace, using God's word and according to God's timing.

Theologically compromised churches need to be brought back to the scriptures. A replanter is not free to compromise the historic gospel but the manner and timing of working through theological issues must be governed by the Holy Spirit, love and mission.

In addition, the replanter must not jump to the conclusion that the obvious solution is for this church to leave the denomination. This is a much more complicated question that needs to be wisely addressed. This is one topic where a mature coach is needed to help a replanter think through all the historical, social, theological and missional implications.

The call by God to replant/revitalize a church is significant and wonderful. Jesus loves his bride and desires her wellbeing. Yet a call to replant a church is also a difficult call. Thus, confirming a call by God to be a replanter needs to be undergirded by prayer and the best training/coaching available.

An evangelical replant pastor, like a missionary, needs to embrace the preparation required for going in to another culture. It takes time and effort but it is time and effort well spent. This cultural training is in addition to the normal preparation required for pastoring a church, such as seminary or other forms of formal education.

New pastors often underestimate the practical, shepherding, and political skillsets needed to lead a church, especially in a replanting context. Good preparation and coaching, both theological and pastoral, helps prevent surprises and the foolish mistakes often made by a rookie pastors.

The call to be a church replanter is also a call to be a good leader. At the beginning of a church revitalization effort much of the work falls on the pastor. The pastor's ability to lead and manage the rebuilding effort has a significant impact on the success or failure of that endeavor. While it is God alone who changes people and builds the body spiritually, He typically works through gifted leaders.[15]

It takes work and time for any pastor to become a skilled leader. While leadership skills are partly innate and partly learned, they must be developed. Future pastors need to apply themselves to the task of developing leadership and interpersonal skills. Honing these leadership skills should be a standard part of coaching for seminary students. It can't be done in the classroom alone, it requires training within a live ministry context.

A leader of the church must think biblically and know how to implement a vision. This includes having a sensitivity for timing and pace, so that changes and new ideas are implemented at an appropriate pace for the congregation not according to the zeal of the replanter.

---

[15] Ephesians 4:11-16.

The ultimate example of leadership in the church is Jesus. Jesus modeled a leadership style which is best described as servant leadership.

Being a servant leader requires fulfilling two roles:

- *A visionary role:* setting the course and the destination.
- *An implementation role:* doing the right things right, with the right timing, combined with a focus on serving.[16]

One blessing of the "honeymoon" period of a new pastorate is it gives the replanter time to serve and transition to a position of earned leadership. Gaining this earned leadership position means personally developing in these leadership roles. It usually requires a two-pronged approach of training and coaching. The replanter would be wise to obtain both.

First, the visionary role starts with seminary training to help a pastor learn to think biblically about all aspects of the ministry in the context of a local church. Good leadership begins with good vision built on a biblical framework.

Mentoring/coaching is also needed to sharpen a pastor's biblical understanding of how their theology actually plays out in a local church.[17] A pastor needs a coach to help him or her wrestle

---

[16] Ken Blanchard and Phil Hodges, *Lead Like Jesus*, (Nashville, Thomas Nelson, 2005), 84.

[17] Tim Keller in *Center Church* calls this one's "theological vision." Pastors need to do the hard work of developing a "faithful restatement of the gospel with rich implications for life, ministry, and mission in their culture at this moment of history." It is how one's sees their theology playing out in a given culture. Tim Keller, Center Church (Grand Rapids, MI, Zondervan, 2012), 20.

with whether the nuances of their vision and proposed implementation plans are faithful to scripture and biblical wisdom. They need a coach who will personally interact with them on their thinking and plans.[18] Having an ongoing dialogue with an experienced veteran pastor who can ask pointed questions is critical. This iron-sharpens-iron approach to pastoral preparation pays great dividends.

Second, the implementation role requires a good leadership skillset. A pastor's ability to be a good leader is a critical component to a successful church replanting effort. Serious attention and effort needs to be applied by the church replanter in order to grow in these necessary leadership skill sets.

Again, coaching is a critical component. A young leader can't lead and simultaneously evaluate how they are leading. A budding leader needs to find someone to observe them as they go through the process of leading and implementing their plans in order to get first hand feedback and critique.[19] Eventually, there are often lay leaders who can help fulfill this roll. Once you have healthy leaders in the church, the replanter will need to recruit them to participate in this process. However, in the beginning years of a replant, it is usually best to leverage an outside resource for coaching,

Another helpful component for becoming a good leader is to learn from the examples of other good leaders, both historical[20] and

---

[18] DA Carson once commented to me at a pastor's conference in 1998 that true education requires that the student be able to interact with someone smarter and more experienced than themselves, if they are going to truly learn something.
[19] This is obviously difficult when the pastor's coach is also a pastor, since they will typically be ministering at the same time. Effective coaching will require some creativity, such as leveraging technology or having gifted lay people observe.
[20] Biographies are a great way to see the long term effect of various leadership decisions and styles. One great book on leadership in general is *Band of Rivals*,

present day, as well as Christian and non-Christian. Good examples give a future leader a picture of what he or she is trying to attain. Church replanting and revitalization is nothing new. It has been going on since shortly after the New Testament church started. A church replanter would do well to learn from the cloud of witnesses that has gone before them.

The church has over the centuries continued to decline and by God's grace revive. We have good examples of church replanters from every century since the church began. In recent history, you could point to John Owen of the eighteenth century, A.J. Gordon of the nineteenth century and Dr. Harold Ockenga of the twentieth century. It is my prayer that you the reader will be an example from the twenty-first century.

One critical source for examples of leading revival is in the scriptures. In the remaining chapters, we will be focusing on the book of Nehemiah, which chronicles God's call of Nehemiah and the leadership skills he demonstrated in the rebuilding of the city of Jerusalem. Nehemiah provides us with a great example of how to lead a replanting/revitalization effort within a challenging community of believers.

As we walk with Nehemiah, we will discover fourteen principles of leadership[21] from Nehemiah's experience revitalizing the city of Jerusalem. We will follow him as God calls him, as he

---

which is about President Lincoln's ability to humbly recruit other great leaders and mold them into a functioning team.

[21] I was advised that fourteen principles was too many. However, renewal is neither simple nor easy. There are probably more than fourteen principles at work in the book of Nehemiah. It didn't seem fair to you, the replanter, to whittle the number down. But as they say, the proof is in the pudding and you the reader can decide if I was wrong.

responds to that call, as he begins the revitalization project, how he responds to pushback, adjustments Nehemiah makes as the project moves from physical reconstruction to civic reconstruction, and his ongoing work of revitalization.

Let's begin our journey alongside Nehemiah.

CHAPTER 2
BEING CALLED OF GOD

Consultant	I would let those churches die. Why waste money on trying to help those dead entities.
Overseed Director	So are you saying, just let them go to Hell? They are not worth the effort?
Jesus	*Go therefore and make disciples of all the nations* (including the faded little map dots[22] of New England), *baptizing them in the name of the Father and the Son and the Holy Spirit, teaching them to observe all that I commanded you; and lo, I am with you always, even to the end of the age.*[23]

---

[22] Lyric from Kenny Chesney song *American Kids*. Writer(s): Luke Robert Laird, Shane L. Mcanally Copyright: Smack Ink, Twangin And Slangin Songs, Songs Of Universal Inc., Creative Nation Music, Universal Music Corp.
[23] Matthew 28:19-20.

2 – BEING CALLED OF GOD

Foundational to taking on the task of replanting a church is the call of God. Despite the tremendous outreach potential in a community through a church replant, typically the work is too hard, the resulting conflict is too draining, and the duration of the project is too long to be sustained by any earthly motivation. It requires the replanter to be crystal clear about God's call on his/her life.

Nehemiah had a great secular job. He was the cup bearer for King Artaxerxes in the 5th century BC. It was a position of influence and prestige. He had regular access to the king and the queen as cup bearer. It was a position of great trust because the life of the king was in his hands, since poisoning was a common means for disposing of those in power.

At the height of his secular career, Nehemiah was called of God for a different purpose. This call of God came first as a heavy burden on Nehemiah's heart over the great distress and reproach of the remnant living around Jerusalem. This call was then confirmed by a season of intensive prayer.

A LEADER MUST CARE

The chronicle of Nehemiah's leadership of this great replanting/revitalization effort in Jerusalem and his call by God begins with Nehemiah's heart.[24] He cared. The text says in Nehemiah 1:4 that when Nehemiah heard the news of the hardships in Jerusalem he wept and mourned for days.

---

[24] Nehemiah 1:1-4.

Jerusalem was not some exciting building project that caught Nehemiah's attention. He cared about the wellbeing of his brothers and sisters back home. He cared about God's glory. He hurt for the Jewish nation as a whole. Nehemiah was deeply touched by the bad news he heard because he loved Jerusalem and his people. His distress was too great to be relieved by one outburst of tears.[25]

The call to be a pastor is first of all a call to love a group of people whom God has assembled in a particular place for the duration of the call. The ministry requires a dynamic skill set, but as Paul explains in 1 Corinthians 13, the greatest attribute you can bring to the ministry is love. It is love, both grace and truth,[26] merged into a single being that results in an incarnational approach to ministry, a ministry style that reflects the person of Jesus Christ to the church. It is a love the moves the replanter to preach Christ crucified and personally live out Christ crucified.

To love people who are needy sinners is one of the great challenges of being a pastor. Pastors have to embrace the ministry perspective that those in the church are not a burden to endure but are a people to love.

Leighton Ford comments on how it changed his view of ministry when he realized that Jesus never viewed people as interruptions, even though people were constantly pushing themselves into the midst of his ministry. Dr. Ford realized that these people who he had viewed as interruptions had been sent to him by God and that he needed to regain a shepherd's vision. The

---

[25] Loring W. Batten, *The Books of Ezra and Nehemiah*, International Critical Commentary, ed. C. A. Briggs, S. R. Driver, and A. Plumer (New York, NY: Charles Scribner's Sons, 1913), 185.
[26] John 1:14.

bottom line of the pastorate is not the work to be done but the pastor's love for his/her people.[27]

Dr. Bob Thompson, a UCC church replanter from North Carolina, shares that central to his call to be a replanter in a theologically compromised historic church was the realization that there were God's people in these churches who needed a shepherd. His concern over the theological direction of a particular denomination didn't mitigate that need. He found he was free to pastor an individual congregational church as God directed, while learning how to love other colleagues with different theological frameworks.

Love is the mark of being a disciple of Christ[28] and is also God's desired outcome for each church. The true mark of success in any church is that the members are truly loving each other and those in their community.[29]

There are many other responsibilities that make up the job description of a pastor but none is more preeminent than the call to love people. This kind of pastoral heart must be acquired. It is only formed by an ongoing personal walk with God in the midst of the crucible of life. Love is an acquired taste.

Over the years as Nehemiah walked and prayed with God, he had grown in his love for God's people. A love for both those that lived locally in Susa and for the far away remnant living in the distant city of Jerusalem. You see a glimpse of this love through the deep sadness he felt in response to the news of their distress.

---

[27] Leighton Ford, *Transforming Leadership*, (Downers Grove, InterVarsity Press, 1991), 208.
[28] John 13:34-35.
[29] Ephesians 4:16.

Nehemiah could not brush off the news that God's people were in a tough spot, especially knowing he could do something about it. He could not move on from this interruption that God brought into his life. Nehemiah's deep and loving concern would eventually transform Jerusalem.

There is no replacement for love; a leader must care.

A LEADER MUST PRAY, ASKING GOD TO CLARIFY THE CALL

Nehemiah was moved to prayer and fasting by this concern for Jerusalem and for the welfare of the people living there.[30] Nehemiah fasted regularly and interacted with God over the duration of roughly three to four months, asking God to rebuild the walls of Jerusalem and reestablish the city. Even though Nehemiah was a great political and military leader, he responded first with prayer. His communion with God was the source of his success[31]

Nehemiah rehearses the character of God as he prays, confesses his sins and those of the people, and reminds God of His promises. At some point in this prayer vigil he begins to realize God is calling him to rebuild Jerusalem. His prayer shifts from asking God to rebuild Jerusalem to asking God to allow him to be successful in rebuilding Jerusalem for God's glory. Nehemiah labors long in prayer before he leads the people in laboring to rebuilding the walls of

---

[30] Nehemiah 1:4-11.
[31] Yosef Rabinowitz, *The Book of Nehemiah*, ed. Nosswon Scherman and Meir Zlotowitzm (Brooklyn, NY: Mesorah Publications, 1990), 35.

Jerusalem. The work of prayer is central to Nehemiah view of the work he is called to do.[32]

He is empowered by his faith in the promises of God.[33] It is during those months of seeking the face of God that God's Spirit speaks to Nehemiah's spirit. Nehemiah believes that God can and will fulfill his promises. During these months of prayer, Nehemiah goes from being merely someone who is concerned about Jerusalem to being the one called by God to go to Jerusalem and to lead this revitalization effort.[34]

Leading any work begins with first getting God's perspective and calling clear. This takes time. But it is necessary time because the leader must seek God's will concerning both the problems and the various opportunities presenting themselves. We see this consistent pattern in both the Old and the New Testaments, leaders begin by seeking the details of God's will before engaging in the work of God.

Paul learned this lesson early in his ministry when his initial attempts at ministry didn't accomplish what he had hoped. Paul was smart, educated, and energetic, yet his initial ministry efforts were ineffective. He needed to go spend time alone with God in Arabia, in order to integrate what he knew in his mind with what he had experienced in his heart.

---

[32]Derek Kidner, *Ezra and Nehemiah, An introduction and* Commentary, vol. 11 of Tyndale Old Testament Commentaries, edited by D. J. Wiseman, (Downers Grove, IL: Inter-Varsity Press, 1969), 78-79.

[33] J. McConville, *Ezra, Nehemiah and Esther* (Philadelphia, PA: The Westminster Press, 1985), 4.

[34] Our prayers are often not specifically about the call but rather about the concerns that God lays upon the leader's heart. It is in the midst of asking God to address our concern that God's call becomes apparent.

Paul experienced a transformation as he surrendered to God and to God's plan for him. Paul grew in his trust of God's presence and provision. He grew confident in God's unconditional love as he abided in Jesus. Only then was he prepared to return to Damascus to effectively teach and equip the church.[35]

The crucial question is not, "can I do this ministry?" but rather "does God want me to do this ministry?" Certainly, part of answering this question of calling is understanding how God has gifted someone, but gifting alone doesn't equate to calling.

Charles Spurgeon identified four aspects of a true call of God to the ministry, which are still applicable today:[36]

1. **Compulsion:** The first sign of God's call to the ministry as an intense, all-absorbing desire for the work. Those called by God to the ministry of being a Senior Pastor sense a growing compulsion to preach, teach and shepherd the people of God.
2. **Competency:** There must be some aptness to teach and some measure of the other qualities for the office.
3. **Conversion:** There must be a measure of conversion-work going on under the effort of those called to the ministry.
4. **Confirmation:** The agreement of the church after prayerful judgment. One's preaching should be acceptable to the people of God.

---

[35] K. Blanchard and P. Hodges, *Lead Like Jesus* (Nashville, TN: Thomas Nelson, 2005), 23.
[36] Charles Spurgeon, *Lectures to my Students* (Grand Rapids, MI, 1995), 23-30.

A clear & biblical sense of call is vitally important. If one is foggy about the calling to be a replanter, then one will also be foggy about whether God is calling he/she to stay, especially if the going gets tough.

For example, if the sole foundation of one's calling is only ability, then difficulty can easily be viewed as a sign that one is no longer capable and is therefore a negation of the call. This sort of confusion over the call can end up undermining the long term work of replanting. Difficulty is usually just part of the process of revitalization and leaving can seriously undercut the work God is doing.

Again, it is not "do I want to do this ministry" but rather it is "does God want me to do this ministry?" It is important for a pastor to be excited about the church and its ministry goals, objectives, and strategies. However, the work itself will rarely motivate one to finish the race, especially if one faces strong opposition to those ministry plans.

As the costs increase, it typically gets harder and harder for the replanter to justify the effort and personal sacrifice. If one is to persevere and fulfill their ministry, one must first know the will and call of God. This call is only discovered as the leader prays and waits on God to confirm the call and timing of that call.[37]

---

[37] Nehemiah's sensitivity to God's timing may be beyond what is recorded. The king, having been prejudiced against Jerusalem by the cunning of Rehum and his friends in Samaria, had put a stop to the previous attempt at fortifying Jerusalem. In the meantime, there had recently been a serious rebellion in Egypt and the providence beyond the river, which probably motivated the King to desire a stable and friendly Jerusalem. Nehemiah may have capitalized on the current historical events, which aided his securing authorization to rebuild the walls of Jerusalem. [McConville, *Ezra, Nehemiah and Esther*, 79-80].

As with all God's laborers, God has been preparing a replant pastor over the course of his/her lifetime. Much has to take place to get a replanter into the pulpit.[38] Education, coaching, and ministry involvement over the years all play a role in preparing a replanter to lead the effort. There is nothing the enemy would like more than to sabotage a replant in its infancy. Satan has a better shot at derailing a replant if the replanter is fuzzy on the call.

Yes, there is a huge need for pastors to shepherd theologically compromised, declining churches in America. Barna's latest poll shows that New England is the most unchurched area of the United States, all the while probably having the greatest number of physical church buildings.[39] One viable strategy for reaching New England communities for Christ is via replanting these declining, theologically compromised historic churches. As in New Testament times, there is always the ongoing need to both plant and replant churches in America. It is not either/or but rather both/and.

Yet, need alone doesn't constitute call. The potential replant pastor needs to pray and ask God where God is calling him or her to serve and in what context. Like Nehemiah, a leader must pray and ask God to clarify the call. The author's advice would be to not take on such a challenging and difficult ministry setting, especially if there is a family involved, without being clear of God's call.

---

[38] Dave Jewitt describes how God uses the opportunities we've pursued, the interests we've had, the positions we've held, the things we've tried, our accomplishments and failures, and our responses to our life's situations to prepare and guide us toward His calling on our lives. [Dave Jewitt, *Your One Degree Participant Handbook*, 2013, 10].

[39] Frank Newport, http://www.gallup.com/poll/160415/mississippi-maintains-hold-religious-state.aspx, 2/13/20013.

Overseed has developed a profile of church replanter. It was one of the outcomes of a yearlong replanter roundtable lead by the author with fifteen experienced replanters at Gordon Conwell Theological Seminary. The replanter profile is located in Appendix A.

It has been the experience of Overseed that those replanters who possess the majority of these traits have found great joy and God given success in replanting churches. If you are sensing God's call on your life to replant, the next step is to begin responding to that call.

CHAPTER 3

RESPONDING TO GOD'S CALL

Author pondering "should a church stay or leave the UCC?"

Is the decision to serve in a historic mainline[40] denomination a moral or a missional question? Is it sinful to take a pastoral position in a mainline church, or can it be a strategic move for the sake of mission and reaching a local community for Christ? I submit it is missional!

Ed Stetzer:

Missional is a Christian term that describes a lifestyle of living as a sent one. Living missionally is to identify with and join God in his mission, which Jesus explained was to seek, to save, to serve others. Those who are living missionally are seeking to do the same in the name of Christ. [41]

---

[40] "Mainline" churches refers to the following group of churches: American Baptist, Disciples of Christ, Episcopal Church USA, Evangelical Lutheran Church, Presbyterian Church USA, United Church of Christ, and the United Methodist Church. The term appears to have first been used to refer to these historic churches that were along the main railroad track.

[41] Ed Stetzer, What is a missional church?, Ed Stetzer - Lifeway Research Blog, Lifeway Research, http://www.edstetzer.com/2010/02/what-is-a-missional-church.html (accessed on February 3, 2010)].

3 – Responding to God's Call

As the call of God begins to crystalize for Nehemiah, God empowers him to begin strategizing about how to address the problems in Jerusalem. Leadership requires being intentional in response to God's call.

A Leader Must Plan

Nehemiah responded to God's call by developing a plan of action as he prayed and reflected on the situation in Jerusalem.[42] This time of preparation allowed Nehemiah to be prepared to lead once God gave him the opportunity. When the King inquired as to what was bothering Nehemiah in chapter two, Nehemiah was prepared to engage the King about the current state of affairs in Jerusalem, what God was calling him to do, and how he planned to proceed.

At some point during the four prior months, as Nehemiah fasted and prayed, God communicated that Nehemiah was to go to Jerusalem personally and lead the rebuilding effort. Nehemiah used the remaining time to continue to prepare and think through the details of how to launch such a rebuilding effort.

As far as we know, Nehemiah had no experience in construction but when the time came for action he knew what to do. He either got the training he needed in those initial months or the scriptures are silent on how God had previously prepared him for this calling.

---

[42] Nehemiah 2:1-6.

Nehemiah also mentally prepared for what he hoped would be an eventual opportunity to discuss his plans with the King and to request a temporary leave of absence from his current position to go lead this renewal effort in Jerusalem. He estimated how long it would take to rebuild the wall. He researched and identified what resources he would need, thought through how the funding would work, and any other resources he would need.

The author remembers the first time a large donor asked what I expected of giving partners. I responded with my best "deer in the headlights" look. You rarely get two shots at people of wealth, power and influence. You need to prepare and think through the details of the plan, so you can honor God with how you handle the opportunity.

The leader must not shrink back in fear when the moment of God's timing appears but rather boldly engage the opportunity to begin enacting the plan as God leads. Though Nehemiah is afraid he does not shrink back or hesitate to engage the King over his request. The moment of Nehemiah's opportunity was fearful, for a servant was not to bring his personal problems to work or to reveal them in the King's presence. To do so might bring punishment or even banishment from the royal presence. [43]

When God gave Nehemiah an opportunity to address the King, Nehemiah was ready because he had taken the time to think through the details of the project. He had a command of both the big picture and of the details. Leadership requires a patient intentionality.

---

[43] Batten, *The Books of Ezra and Nehemiah*, 191.

If you have ever watched the TV show "Shark Tank[44] you get a picture of what it is like to have one shot in front of someone who can help make your dream come true. Unfortunately, what often transpires in the course of the show is that these four multi-millionaire business gurus quickly uncover that the plans of those who are seeking funding have not been well thought through. They may have a great idea, but the details of the business proposition often falls flat on its face.

Nehemiah had one shot to convince the King of the value of his plan and that he could indeed pull it off. Nehemiah would have only one opportunity to obtain the King's blessing to invest kingdom resources in this project. Their discussion would have probably made a great season finale for Shark Tank.

Leadership requires a patient intentionality and a key part of that patient intentionality is planning. Planning is an ongoing part of pastoral leadership. Leaders have to plan, plan again, and re-plan. Church leaders need to make planning a regular part of their schedule.

Sometimes committees/ministry teams have trouble coming up with good ideas because lay leaders do not have the time to think through all the particulars surrounding an issue/opportunity. One of the responsibilities of the fulltime pastor is to continually clarify the vision and take the time to think through the implication of the church's vision to the issues at hand. As a result, he or she can then

---

[44] *Shark Tank* is a business themed reality series featuring the sharks -- tough, self-made, multi-millionaire and billionaire tycoons – who give budding entrepreneurs the chance to make their dreams come true and potentially secure business deals that could make them millionaires. CNBC, http://www.cnbc.com/id/101229255?__source=pd|sharktank|Google&par=pd/, March 29, 2014.

offer up good ideas to leadership teams allowing the teams to administrate, massage, and improve upon the initial ideas.

One speaker's concluding application to his message from a conference I attending during my college days was "Prior Preparation Prevents Poor Performance." There is a lot of truth in that small saying. In a replant situation, this preparation needs to begin with the pastor. A replant pastor may not be gifted in administration but in the early stages of a replant the planning is still going to fall to the pastor. A replant pastor may need to recruit administrative help or get coaching in order to improve their planning skills.

In a replanting context, there are two major areas that the replanter and appropriate ministry teams must continually wrestle with in order to avoid poor performance as a team.

1) Planning what is required for the various aspects of the ministry to move forward.
2) Planning for how the church should respond to various problems that surface in midst of ministry.

Both areas require problem-solving, decision-making skills and action steps to move beyond the problem/opportunity to the resolution/implementation.

In addition to those two, the replanter also has to think through pace. In the early days of a replant, a lot of things are typically broken and you can't fix everything at once. So the challenge is determining which issues to address and how fast does the replanter or team need to address a particular issue.

For example, it is not unusual for a replanter, upon coming to a historic New England, to find people in positions of leadership or ministry who are living in open sin. Often this is because the congregation doesn't have a good grasp of the bible, and therefore they aren't aware that God has prohibited a certain behavior. Thus, you can't address sin before you define sin from the scriptures. It may take a year or two of preaching the historic gospel before someone begins to question so and so's behavior. Repairing the foundations is messy time consuming work.

This messy work requires living with tension and a ton of grey. Few issues are black and white in the mind of the congregation. Replanters are easily tempted to either ignore issues or resolve them too quickly. Maintaining a balance requires much wisdom on the part of the replanter. The ongoing planning process is one significant reason for a young church replanter to get coaching,

Problem solving is an inherent part of the decision making process. Unfortunately, "results oriented" people tend to find the process of thinking through a problem difficult and boring. They just want to jump ahead and prematurely decide something. They want to stay away from this difficult work of problem solving and thus they can make poor decisions.

A problem/opportunity by definition presents certain alternatives. The team, or a subset of the team, has to take the time and mental energy to sort out these possible solutions and evaluate the feasibility of each one. The failure to embrace the difficulty of deferring judgment until thinking through the options often results in early and often unwise decisions.[45]

Leadership requires a patient intentionality. In addition to planning, patient intentionality requires developing and refining the organizational infrastructure.

For example, a replanter will probably need to help the board or leadership team rethink through the process of how a team/committee/board will vote. This will require the team to think through how the church wants to balance the wisdom of each leader, the collective wisdom of the team, and the amount of time being spent on any particular decision.

Some local churches place the emphasis on the team and thus have chosen the democratic approach, where simple majority rules the day. This simplifies the process and keeps the decision making process moving forward. The negatives of this democratic approach is that the decision making process can become highly political and run roughshod over individuals, move too quickly, and miss God's will. Over time the boards often attract either very domineering personalities or passive aggressive political people. The natural leaders are often frustrated and are no longer willing to serve.

Other churches are more concerned with not making any leadership mistakes and do not want to minimize God's ability to speak through each leader on the committee. They take the opposite approach and require that all decisions be unanimous. The negative of this approach is it often leads to a long drawn out

---

[45] Kenn Gangel, *Coaching Ministry Teams,* Swindoll Leadership Library, ed. by Charles Swindoll and Roy Zuck (Nasville, TN: Word Publishing, 2000), 32.

decision making process on non-critical items, which hamstring the church's ability to move forward because a decision is held hostage by one person's pet peeve. Thus, the natural leaders often get frustrated and no longer are willing to serve.

Over time both of these approaches can lead to frustrating board meetings.

A third methodology is a hybrid of the two. Every decision is first decided to be either critical or non-critical. Non-critical decisions are decided by simple majority, whereas critical decisions are determined by unanimity. A decision is declared critical by simple majority. Unfortunately, regardless of voting methodology some board meetings will still have their frustrating moments.

It will always take regular planning on the leader's part to wisely lead teams in the ongoing task of future planning and problem solving. This planning needs to include both long range planning on a yearly basis as well as week to week short range planning. A leader must plan, re-plan, and plan again. It is an ongoing process and a regular part of the job.

A LEADER UNDERSTANDS THE IMPORTANCE OF POSITION

A good leader understands that position is often a necessary part of God's call to lead. Position is certainly not to be the means to lord authority over people.[46] However, for the replanter to serve the congregation as a whole, especially in the early stages of a replant, position is often a necessary tool. This was a lesson that Nehemiah

---

[46] 1 Peter 5:1-3.

had learned in the Persian court. "As the cup bearer he occupied a position of immense influence within the Empire because of his closeness to the king ... and thus perfectly placed to lay the petitions of his Jewish brethren before the highest authority." [47]

Nehemiah understood the importance of position.[48] Nehemiah needed to establish himself as the new governor appointed by the King, because he knew his plan to rebuild the walls was going to incite displeasure among God's enemies.[49] Along these lines, Nehemiah requested a military escort, which was probably intended to intimidate Nehemiah's enemies[50] and probably contributed to them resorting to bluff instead of force in their early opposition to him.[51]

Being a pastor is different and yet, most people do respond differently to someone who holds a position of authority.[52] Most replants face opposition, and position can be helpful in addressing dysfunctional patterns of leadership opposition. The challenge facing the pastor is how to lead from the position without lording it over those in the congregation, without manipulating people or using the position for selfish goals.

---

[47] McConville, *Ezra, Nehemiah and Esther*, 74.

[48] Nehemiah 2:9.

[49] There is certainly a difference between being a pastor and being a civic governor, but there is also overlap to all leadership positions.

[50] The guard was of considerable size, since it consisted of officers and cavalry. [Batten, *The Books of Ezra and Nehemiah*, 195].

[51] There was more than protection to be gained from the military escort. It meant arriving in style, impressively reinforcing the presentation of credentials to the neighboring governors, and making very plain the change of royal policy. [Kidner, *Ezra and Nehemiah*, 1979), 81].

[52] It appears probable that the reason Ezra was not able to make progress on rebuilding the wall was the lack of royal authority and by extension military might. [Rabinowitz, *The Book Of Nehemiah*, 33-34].

In the TV show *Blue Bloods,* Tom Selleck plays the role of New York police commissioner. His character often clashes with the will of the city mayor. In an early episode, when the police commissioner refuses to do what the mayor wants, the mayor reminds him that he works for him. The police commissioner responds that he does not work for the mayor, only at the pleasure of the Mayor. In other words, you can relieve me of my position but you can't tell me how to run my office.

Pastors are in a similar situation. They are called of God and do not "work" for the church. The church can release the pastor from office but can't view him/her as an employee.[53] This is a problem in many New England churches. Often the pastor has been viewed as an employee for a long time and it is challenge to help them reframe the pastor position biblically.

Despite these potential landmines, it is not an option for the pastor to shrink back from leadership. Rather the replant pastor needs to emulate Jesus' model of being a servant leader.[54]

In an excellent paper entitled "The Institution as Servant," Robert Greenleaf writes about the importance of servant leadership:

The traditional view understands the modus operandi[55] of the institution in three parts, but with one overarching element:

1. *Goals and Strategy,* including long-range thinking that culminates in plans.

---

[53] *Blue Bloods,* CBS.
[54] Mark 10:45. [Ford, *Transforming Leadership,* 1991), 153-154].
[55] *Modus operandi* is a Latin phrase, approximately translated as "method of operation." In this case, it is the usual way of functioning as an institution.

2. *Organization,* the concern with people and structure, the reasonably durable arrangements, and the staffing for carrying out plans.

3. *Implementation,* the day-to-day execution of plans, including administrative initiative and response to situations. It is the use made of the organization to carry out the plans.

Overarching these three is the exercise of *leadership,* which gives the total process coherent and dynamic force by establishing priorities, allocating resources, choosing and guiding staff, articulating goals and philosophy, and exerting a sustained goal for excellency.

Then Greenleaf goes on to point out how in the second part, the organization, is the curiously neglected element. Any apparent concern with the organization is typically superficial and unaddressed. He suggests one reason may be because of an intuitive sense that the trouble lies hidden here and that we had best leave it alone.[56]

Organization has to do with people, whom the bible tells us are sinners. Shepherding sinners is a difficult calling and requires that one take up their cross and follow Christ. As Jesus pointed out, the organizational difficulties can be met in the typically worldly way by lording it over people, or leaders can choose to serve, shepherding those in their care, proving to be examples to the church.[57]

---

[56] Robert K. Greenleaf, *The Institution as Servant* (Westfield, IN: 2009), 18-19.
[57] 1 Peter 5:1-3.

Organizationally, the replanter needs to understand where the people are at. He/she also needs to help the people understand where they are at and what are the implications of the present situation and thinking. For example, dysfunctional people often like dysfunction. Thus visitors who keep coming back may not be attracted to the replanter's vision but rather to current dysfunction in the environment.

Addressing organizational challenges takes leadership. The challenge is how to actually go about leading. The answer is somewhat determined by the context. In healthy organizations, there is rarely a need for the leader to have to leverage his position in order to lead. However, in an unhealthy or dysfunctional church family one may find that leveraging the role of position may sporadically be necessary when beginning such a pastorate. This is further complicated in New England as many dislike authority. It is not personal, they are just oppositional. Thus, the use of position in historic New England churches must be only used rarely and wisely.

Any leader who is lording his position over the flock is missing how God calls a pastor to lead the church. However, a highly dysfunctional church which is made up of mostly unbelievers is going to attempt to manage the church by politics. As a result, a replanter may need to play a political card or two in the right circumstances as guided by the Holy Spirit.

Many replants of stage four churches (those in serious decline)[58] often have a matriarch/patriarch who have a history of

---

[58] The author interviewed twenty-five experienced replant pastors and developed a chart to help a young pastor identifying the level of decline in a church. The chart is meant to be a quick analysis of a church to determine

61

opposing pastors, running pastors out, and forcing their will upon the congregation. Wise use of position can help break this historic dysfunction in a particular church. A wise leader understands the purpose of all the tools in his toolbox, when to use each one and how to use each one.

One benefit to position is that it often helps the leader build bridges of communication faster with those in the church. Most people want the input of the leader and desire a relationship with him or her. As a result, the leader often starts further down the path of relationship with people. This allows the leader to spread his time around to more people, since the typical amount of time required to build trust is not as long.

However, this also requires discipline on the leader's part to know when he or she should take the time to listen to people in order to get to know them deeper. A pastor who is a natural leader, needs to be careful to not allow themselves to become merely functional or manipulative with people.

A new leader also needs to take into consideration the existing leadership structure, including the informal leaders. Nehemiah, where possible, used existing leaders or people of influence as his supervisors for rebuilding the various sections of the wall. This enabled Nehemiah to enlist the aid of these leaders in

---

how bad it is, i.e. what is the starting point of the replant? The chart is in Appendix B.

recruiting other workers, since they already had respect and authority in the community.[59]

Often in a replant situation, the existing leadership was selected without regard to their leadership abilities or biblical character qualifications. Especially in small churches, leaders are typically selected because they were the only ones willing to serve. Often when a replanter arrives at the church, the leadership board(s), such as the elders or deacons, have a majority of unspiritual people as members.

In order to move the church forward the replanter is going to need to raise the leadership qualification bar. This is a delicate issue in that it often means that existing leaders are displaced due to being unqualified. The difficulty of removing them is compounded by the fact that it is these leaders who have kept the church from closing. These leaders may need to be moved to others areas where they are qualified but the process of removing them must be done with dignity and honor.[60]

Removing existing leaders is a process covered with hidden landmines. It is easy for a new pastor to overestimate their influence and to underestimate the influence of others. Many a pastor has been shown the door when trying to remove unqualified leaders. It requires timing, patience, and much wisdom and counsel.

---

[59] Alison Barfoot, *Principles of Empowerment from the Book of Nehemiah: A Leadership Training Program*, (Charlotte, NC: Gordon-Conwell Theological Seminary, 1999), 73.
[60] These existing leaders often make life very difficult for a replanter in the early years of a replant. The replanter needs to keep working at forgiving, loving and honoring those leading the church when he/she arrived.

Rev. Dr. Bob Thomson, a veteran church replanter from North Carolina, experienced firsthand how raising the qualification bar of leadership is often a slow process in a replant situation. He recommends developing a method to discern which members have greatest trust from most people to help get the church moving in this direction. He found that a simply survey worked very well in his context.

His recommended method for selecting initial leaders in a replant situation is as follows:

- Set in motion some process for forming a strategy committee.
- Open up nominations to any name suggested by anyone in the congregation, and include all current elected office holders.
- Submit this large list of nominees to a secret ballot vote to either the entire congregation or to an official board or committee (depending on polity). Ask voters to mark all names they would have confidence in to be part of this evaluation and planning process. They may mark as few or as many names in whom they have confidence.
- Then ask the top vote getters who fit the basic biblical qualifications above to form the strategy team. Also consider balance (gender, age, length of time in the congregation, etc) as you decide who should be on the team.

In addition, this has to be accompanied with biblical teaching on the different qualifications for leadership, including why such qualifications are important and necessary. Our pragmatic, compartmentalized culture often fails to understand why qualifications other than pragmatic skillsets matter. They need to be taught why the scriptures teach that what one does in private affects their qualification for public service, especially since the culture is telling them that it doesn't matter. This process can takes several years for the congregation to truly grasp what the scriptures are teaching.

One reason President Clinton was not impeached over the Monica Lewinsky scandal is that the country could not grasp why private morality mattered for public service. Engaging in sex outside of marriage was no longer seen as an important disqualification for a president. If these kind of moral issues do not matter in such a critical political context, it is not difficult to understand why people might assume it does not matter for someone taking on a leadership position in a small church. However, the scriptures are clear that morality does indeed matter.

Leadership requires being intentional about the ministry in response to God's call. This is true both before the replanter gets to the church and once he/she is there. The replanter will need to be intentional about preparing, planning and carrying out his/her position.

Oftentimes, a replanter's position of pastor can be a helpful tool in helping to address overly controlling dysfunctional behavior. In addition, building trust with existing leaders extends the influence through their network of relationships.

Once the call is clear and God has led a replanter to replant a declining historical church, the next question is, "Where does one start?" How do you even determine what is the starting point? How does the replanter go about beginning the change process in order to move an existing church from dysfunction to health? Where does he or she start? Who will be onboard with moving forward with changes and who will be opposed to new ideas? How do you respond to those who disagree?

Nehemiah faced the same kinds of questions as he rode into the broken down city of Jerusalem. It would be most interesting to know what occupied Nehemiah's thoughts during those days as he journeyed from King's palace to Jerusalem. My guess is that he spent much of the time thinking about the challenges that lay ahead of him.

Chapter 4
Beginning the Change Process

Author: So what exactly were you thinking?

Replanter: Not sure, it just seemed like a good idea at
              the time.

Author: Next time, consider developing an actual
              plan first.

4 – Beginning the Change Process

God's call to Nehemiah was clear. God had opened significant doors for Nehemiah. God had appointed him as governor[61] and provided resources for the rebuilding project. But none of this guaranteed that the people would follow Nehemiah. He still needed to recruit those in Jerusalem and in the surrounding community to this vision that God had given him.

Nehemiah had worked in the palace, surrounded by power seeking people at every level of the kingdom administrative engine. Politics were the name of the game. Everywhere. Nehemiah had the unique privilege of regular access to the King, which allowed him to get the King's take on the various events of leading the kingdom. Nehemiah knew first hand that just because you are in power doesn't mean the people are naturally going to follow you. There will be pushback and competing ideas. There will be those seeking to support you and others seeking to overthrow you.

Nehemiah had a good idea of what he was walking into. He had done, as we saw in chapter two, a great job of advance planning for this rebuilding project. However, Nehemiah has never actually seen the walls of Jerusalem himself. Everything he knows is only

---

[61] A pastor typically wears the hat of leader, manager, and administrator. These terms can be defined as follows: leadership is "the development and articulation of a shared vision, motivation of those key people without whom that vision cannot become a reality and gaining the cooperation of most of the people involved; management is "doing the right things. Management includes such things as long-range planning, goal-setting, selecting priorities, time management, and budgeting; administration is "doing things right, If there is a deadline, one meets it, if there is a prescribed structure, one has it, if there are stated policies, one keeps them." [Levett H. Weems, Jr., *Church Leadership* (Nashville, TN: Abingdon Press, 1993), p34].

from second hand information. Thus, when Nehemiah gets to Jerusalem, he first verifies his assumptions and his plan with reality, before beginning to implement his plan.

Nehemiah, for all his speed and drive, does not rush into communicating or implementing his action plan.[62] First, Nehemiah takes three days to get settled and rest. Given Nehemiah's intentionality, it appears that he waited three days to avoid undue attention and to allow him some degree of freedom to conduct his activities without unduly arousing the enemies' suspicion.[63] Then, his next step is to validate the plan, making sure second-hand knowledge of the situation at Jerusalem actually matched reality. For three nights, Nehemiah and a few handpicked men check out the situation.

Nehemiah needed to understand the true starting point of this work and validate his plan in order to fill in missing details and make any needed changes before he started. One of the most common mistakes that evangelical replanters make is not understanding the starting point of their new ministry. They assume friendliness means people are onboard with his plans. They assume certain language means people are on board with the biblical message. They move forward but often find out that their assumptions are wrong and their plans meet unnecessary and what appears to be inexplicable opposition. It can take years for the reasons for this disconnect to surface.

Replanters must take the necessary time to do the missional/cultural homework. Some revitalization efforts require the new pastor to observe for an entire year or more to understand the

---

[62] Kidner, *Ezra and Nehemiah*, 82.
[63] Rabinowitz, *The Book Of Nehemiah*, 48.

congregation and to build enough trust to begin implementing changes. It takes time to get the history as one typically only gets it in bits and pieces along the way as the replanter ministers alongside of people. The replanter needs to do the required homework but it simply takes time to get to know people and their culture.

To help replanters with this initial part of this process, Overseed has developed an informal questionnaire and accompanying diagnostic chart. This tool was the outworking of numerous interviews the author had with experienced replanters. The idea behind this tool was to give the potential replanter an initial read on what the starting point may be before accepting a call from a particular church. Certainly once there, the replanter will need to invest more time and effort into understanding the starting point of this particular replant. The tool can be found in Appendix B.

There is not a blue-print for revitalization in the scriptures. There are principles which need to be applied to the particular context in which the replanter is called. H. Williamson points out that the Jewish community did not have a blueprint for restoration, yet the pattern of restoration was far from haphazard. The plan needed to be formulated and adjusted to the context as the work continued.[64]

Nehemiah wanted to validate his plans in order to fill in missing details and make any needed changes before he started. He knew recruiting for this effort could be potentially difficult. He did not want to recruit laborers to an incomplete plan, which might cause them to doubt his leadership ability at the get go.

---

[64] H. G. M. Williamson, *Ezra and Nehemiah*, Old Testament Guides. Ed.R. N. Whybray (Sheffield, England: Sheffield Academic Press, 1987, 1996), 79.

A replant congregation is typically made up of people who are nice, loyal, but often not strategic by nature. Often they are older and have seen many a pastor come and go. These pastors each had a dream and tried to recruit the congregation to the dream but soon the dream died, things stayed the same, the decline continued and the pastor moved. Understandably, they are skeptical of yet a new plan by a new pastor.

Nehemiah probably faced something of the same issue. In the recent past there had been problems getting the temple rebuilt, mainly due to opposition and discouragement over the task. Rebuilding the temple was a much simpler endeavor than rebuilding the entire wall around Jerusalem and the Israelites had struggled with the temple rebuilding project. How did Nehemiah think they were going to rebuild the entire wall around Jerusalem? It is hard to imagine that Nehemiah wasn't reminded of the problems the Israelites faced when attempting to rebuild the temple by those who were not on board with his plans for rebuilding the wall.[65]

He also knew that once the details of the plan were revealed, opposition would begin in earnest. A bogus plan would only give his enemy ammunition to use against Nehemiah. Thus, he validates the plan first and he does so in secret.

Once Nehemiah is convinced his plan is solid he begins to recruit to his vision. Rebuilding a broken down city wall is hard work. You not only have to build and repair the wall, but you also have to

---

[65] In Ezra 1, we find a number of Israelites return to Jerusalem in 536 B.C. However, in Ezra 4, after making a good start on rebuilding the Temple, they become discouraged under opposition, and the work stops until 520 B.C. God sends the prophets Haggai and Zechariah to encourage them. They once again take up the rebuilding project and finally complete it by 516 B.C.

first cart off the old unusable materials. Plus, given the inevitable opposition it was also going to be eventually dangerous.

Nehemiah, probably as he expected, finds that not everyone is onboard with his plan at the start. He knows the rebuilding project would never get off the ground if he waits until everyone agrees to the rebuilding plan. Plus, he knows his plan must have sounded like a pipe dream to some of them. Nevertheless, Nehemiah decides to start the rebuilding project with those who initially responded to God's call and trusts that the others will engage in the work over time.

Nehemiah identifies who is responding to God's call partly by sharing with them God's role in this undertaking. He points out how God had opened doors at every point along the way and how God had given him favor with the King, so that this undertaken was even being supported by the authority of the King.[66]

Nehemiah commences with phase one of his plan once He has some workers recruited to it. The first step of this initial phase was to communicate all the details. He lays out for everyone their roles and makes sure that each one understood their part in the plan.[67] Once the workers knew their exact job and location, the work begins in earnest.

It is interesting that the description of the work begins with the priests rebuilding the sheep gate and dedicating it. It was the gate which provided easy access to the temple and was used to bring

---

[66] [Batten, *The Books of Ezra and Nehemiah*, 202].
[67] The book of Nehemiah never loses sight of who is doing the work, it is the faith community. The lists of names are an important reminder of this truth. The replant pastor must continually acknowledge those engaged in doing the work. [Wijk-Bos, *Ezra, Nehemiah , and Esther,* 1998), 57].

in the sacrificial animals. Nehemiah had the work begin in a manner that visibly demonstrated the spiritual nature of the work. Replanting is a spiritual work. Rebuilding the church is not about saving traditions, the building, etc.[68]

One of the great challenges of leading is communication. Communication in a church replanting effort is often very difficult, since the new lead pastor is an unknown and is unfamiliar with the various players. The replanter often finds him or herself easily misunderstood and/or challenged about perceived motives by the long term members of the congregation, partly because they simply don't know him or her. Many declining churches have had a revolving door of pastors, often unqualified, and their distrust is unfortunately justified by past experiences. This requires a patient loving intentionality on the part of the replanter

Congregants, who can be fearful of a new pastor, often engage in mental acts[69] and make assumptions about what the new pastor is thinking or why he or she is doing something, which are usually wrong. An innocent offer to help can be seen as controlling or heard as a backhanded critique of how they are not doing the work correctly. Listening to someone's idea can be viewed by others as tactic approval of what they personally think is a bad idea. Visiting someone can be seen by others as either favoritism of that person or an indication that this person has a problem. The list goes on and on.

---

[68] Brown, *The Message of Nehemiah*, 1998), 64-65.
[69] Mental acts is the process of trying to perceive what another person is thinking and what is motivating them without actually asking them.

This makes being intentional about how, when, and what you communicate all that more important. Ted Engstrom offers several helpful hints for devising a communication strategy.

- Stop talking. Listen so that you know the objections and the thinking of those in the church family. It also helps to build relationships, which decreases the likelihood of misunderstanding.
- Success in communication depends upon gaining acceptance of what you desire to say. Therefore the communicator must carefully plan both the content and how to articulate the content.
- One of the best ways to gain acceptance is to give meaningful reasons to those being informed.
- Where persuasion is needed, the oral word can be more effective than the printed word. A face-to-face discussion gives an opportunity to observe reaction and to adapt the presentation.
- Keep the channels open both ways by inviting response.
- In planning a communication strategy, always seek more than one method. A meeting reinforced by a letter sent home is more effective than a onetime announcement.
- Communication is not completed until the communicator is certain that his message was received and interpreted accurately. This will require additional dialogue, especially with those you think may disagree with the content.

Taking time for real communication helps to filter out false reasoning (yours and theirs) and helps a leader to make better judgments. It also provides the means of discovering where others are in their feelings, goals and attitudes. It is all too easy for the new pastor to assume that people are onboard with their great new ideas without asking what people actually are thinking and simply launching ahead when the congregation is not with them. [70]

The communication challenge has only increased in complexity in the twenty-first century. A pastor must now adapt to the varied communication methods used by those in the church. Older congregations still tend to prefer a personal phone call or a letter via US Mail, while younger people prefer the proliferating world of text, email, Facebook, Twitter and the like.[71]

Replant pastors who are younger can find it frustrating that older folks don't embrace new technology, which would make the pastor's communication faster and more efficient. Love moves us to bear all things and to move forward with a patient intentionality. The wise replanter also realizes that the face to face time with older saints is worth its weight in gold. It may not be efficient but it is effective. As one coach told me in college, "The fastest way is often not the best way."

A replanter must embrace that the ministry requires a tremendous amount of organizing, scheduling and communicating. These tasks are not occasional onetime events but an ongoing way of life. The cycle of organizing, scheduling and communicating continually repeats itself as the Lord leads the church through various stages of growth and ministry. This is another part of the

---

[70] Ted W.Engstrom, *The Making of a Christian Leader* (Grand Rapids, MI: Zondervan Publishing House, 1976), 156.

[71] While working as a youth pastor in the early 2000's, I had to communicate with students via Facebook and texting, while their parents preferred email or a phone call. The replanter needs to include the delivery method as part of their overall communication plan.

permanent job description that must be owned by the church replanter.[72]

The replanter can't hide behind "that is not my gifting" excuse. The replanter may need to grow in this particular leadership skill set but he/she owns this task.

Peter Scazzero shares how for years how he dodged owning the part of the position. His typical reply to his church board, in their annual review of his role, when asked how he enjoyed his position as senior pastor was:

> "I love preaching, teaching, casting vision, and discipling people," I replied, "But God just didn't give me the gift of administration or managing an organization. It's frustrating." I continued to avoid making personnel decisions, managing staff and key volunteers, writing job descriptions, taking time to plan for meetings, or following through on project details. I saw clearly things that needed to be done but I wanted someone else to do it. "That's not me," I told myself.

However, one year he finally saw things differently:

> Finally, a number of events converged to prepare me for this... I finally admitted the truth: the greatest deterrent to New Life Fellowship Church becoming what God meant her to be was not any other person or factor, but me. ... My avoidance of taking the

---

[72] Raymond Brown summaries the never ending revitalization process cycle as: Replenish Your own resources, Assess needs, Recruit colleagues, Inspire confidence, Handle opposition. [Brown, *The Message of Nehemiah,* 1998), 53-62].

necessary time to plan well or follow through on project details was about my character, not my gift mix. [73]

Nehemiah understood he was called to be the primary leader. Yes, there was much he needed to delegate but one thing he didn't delegate was the key components of his own position.

Leading a church to health means rebuilding the foundations, often like Nehemiah did from the ground up. The replanter must not be in a hurry and simply start somewhere. Rather, it is important for the replanter to seek out God in order to understand what foundational area(s) God wants the replanter to start to work on, what areas can be delegated and what Areas cannot be delegated. Once God has identified the area(s) to begin with, the replanter needs to plan the process well, get the details right, communicate well, and recruit. [74]

As in Nehemiah's experience, not everyone is going to be on board with the plan. Thus, the replanter is going to have to start with those whose hearts God has touched. Renewal is often slow work but the work must be started with those who willing to be a part of the initial work.

In addition to those who are on the fence about the renewal project, there will also be those who are opposed to the idea. Often those in opposition have honed their political skill sets over the years by opposing numerous renewal efforts in the past. Often those in opposition appear to be passive and unengaged but the passivity is

---

[73] Peter Scazzero with Warren Bird, *The Emotionally Healthy Church* (Zondervan, Grand Rapids, MI, 2010), 204, 211.

[74] This is one area where church replanting and church planting have a lot in common.

combined with skillful aggressiveness. Thus, the term that describes most congregants in New England is passive-aggressive.

Many declining churches in New England have had an unintended interim for years as those in opposition continue to oppose renewal efforts and have personally made sure previous pastors moved on to greener pastures. Either they run them off or they quit in frustration.

Passive-aggressive congregants can be a formidable foe to gospel renewal and the wise replanter does the research to make sure he or she understands this common aspect of the New England church culture. The replanter needs to gain a good grasp of what he/she is up against and what are the strategies that God typically uses to address this problem.

Don't misunderstand. Historic New England church congregants are often nice people and care deeply about their church. But unfortunately, their plans and desires for the church will in reality move the church further down the road of decline and are blocking any chance of renewal. It will take wise management, relational savvy and perseverance to lead the church in the process of church revitalization.

Let's learn from Nehemiah's wisdom in how to deal with opposition.

CHAPTER 5

EXPECT PUSHBACK AGAINST CHANGE

Moses:	Doing exactly as God explicitly told him to do
Key Leaders:	Now Korah, ... with Dathan and Abiram, ..., and On ..., took *action*, and they rose up before Moses, together with some of the sons of Israel, two hundred and fifty leaders of the congregation, chosen in the assembly, men of renown. They assembled together against Moses and Aaron, and said to them, "You have gone far enough, for all the congregation are holy, every one of them, and the LORD is in their midst; so why do you exalt yourselves above the assembly of the LORD?
God to leaders:	Epic Fail

5 – EXPECT PUSHBACK AGAINST CHANGE

The plans may be great and the communication strategy flawless, but almost always there will be pushback from some of those affected by the change. Often there is a honeymoon period where the new replant pastor is granted a certain level of freedom and trust to try new things, but sometimes the pushback is immediate.

If God has called you to lead a broken church through change in order to bring about revitalization, then you need to expect that there will be opposition. How the replant pastor responds to opposition often determines the success or failure of the revitalization project. Thus, the replant pastor needs to learn very soon how to respond well to this inevitable opposition to the work of God. Of course, the replanter can't assume that their ideas are God's ideas and the oppositions ideas are not. However, Satan is going to oppose the work of God. It takes walking closely with God to lead according to His will.

As the pastor, you are called to love those in opposition to the replant efforts. Rev. Dr. John Lloyd, an experienced replanter from the south shore of Boston, shares several things that helped him maintain an attitude of love and kindness to those who opposed him.

- Pray for them as it helps me to remember that God loves them. Part of my calling to that church may be to reach them with the gospel.
- Remind myself that people are in different places in their journey.

- Embrace longsuffering, remembering God's long suffering of myself.
- Maintain a constant awareness of my own brokenness and maintain enough transparency that others can remind me.

Not only is the opposition inevitable, but it will often be ongoing and appear to be continual. This was certainly true for Nehemiah. The opposition started in Nehemiah 2:19, continues in 4:1-23 and never ends during his tenure in Jerusalem.

A wise replanter anticipates opposition to change.[75] The temptation for the replanter is to ignore those whom the replanter thinks are going to disagree with the plans because the replanter finds conflict and tension uncomfortable. That would be a serious mistake. One veteran pastor remarked to me that he, as an introvert, he always tried to avoid conflict and so he didn't deal with opposition or other problems until he absolutely had to in his early pastorates. He remarked that he couldn't think of one instance where waiting wasn't a mistake and how waiting only made things worse.

Replanting requires an opposite strategy. The better strategy is for the replanter (or someone on their team) to intentionality stay connected with those who disagree or are likely to disagree with the next required change. A successful Bank Vice President shared with me how he learned early on that the best method of managing people was to keep your enemies close to you. It allows you to know what they are thinking and tends to disarm

---

[75] Nehemiah's call resulted in vocational, geographical, cultural, and social change. He personally could identify with the challenges that change brings. [Brown, *The Message of Nehemiah,* 1998), 26].

84

their behind scenes influence by giving them voice in the process, which means they at some level own responsibility for the eventual decision.

It also means staying connected to those both inside and outside the community, for often opposition will come from both areas. Nehemiah faced opposition from both repeatedly.

The replanter needs to be especially aware of those folks who have left just prior to their arrival or those leaving shortly after their arrival. They have left physically but that doesn't mean their influence has left or that they are not still attempting to control the church from the outside.

This outside opposition can be further complicated by the fact that Satan often blurs the lines of distinction to make identification more difficult. Sanballat, one the key opponents of Nehemiah, appears to have been a Yaweh worshipper given the names of his sons. Nehemiah may have expected collaboration due to religious agreement but Sanballat was more concerned about political realities and was thus committed to compromising Nehemiah and aborting his mission.[76]

Pushback comes for a variety of reasons. Sometimes there is opposition over the details or pace of the plan. However, some people are resistant to change even if they can agree the plan is a good one. Sometimes opposition comes from those who tried

---

[76] Joseph Blenkinsopp, *Ezra-Nehemiah: A Commentary* (Louiseville, KY: Westminster John Knox Press, 1988), 216-217.

before and were thwarted in their efforts and are thus reluctant to try again.[77]

Leighton Ford points out that change inherently involves risk, which threatens one's security. Everyone has a built in resistance to change because it makes us insecure. Change threatens our stability, plus change also threaten one's power and / or position. Thus, even if the current situation is not to one's liking, people will still dig in their heels rather than embrace change.[78]

People who do not want to change typically adopt either a strategy of subtle resistance,[79] or outright opposition to the idea. In both cases, they will begin immediately forming plans to defeat the idea. In a broken church, opposition often doesn't take on a full frontal attack strategy. Folks in a broken church are almost always the more passive/aggressive type, for typically the type "A" leaders have left a long time ago due to frustration at the decline, slow pace of change, and the passive/aggressive type of behavior of other leaders.[80] The replanter needs to be aware that there can be the appearance of agreement from passive/aggressives, while they are fiercely opposing the idea in the background. They end up taking the unaware pastor completely by surprise, which by the way is part of their strategy.

---

[77] George Rawlinson, *Ezra and Nehemiah* (New York, NY: Anson D. F. Randolph and Company, 1890), 120.

[78] Leighton Ford, *Transforming Leadership* (Downers Grove, IL: InterVarsity, 1991), 251.

[79] People in their personal lives usually are free to make their own choices. But in organizations they feel coerced. And so they use the only power they have to regain control: resistance. Peter Bergman, "How to Counter Resistance to Change," The HarvardBuiness.org Voices blog, entry posted April 28, 2009, http://blogs.harvardbusiness.org/bregman/2009/04/how-to-counter-resistance-to-c.html (accessed Nov 21, 2009).

[80] Typically, the only type "A" person that remains is the dysfunctional one who becomes the matriarch or patriarch.

Nehemiah was no stranger to opposition. As soon as his rebuilding plan is communicated to those in Jerusalem, the opposition quickly responded. As the work grew so did the opposition.[81] The opposition tried various tactics to stop the work and to put an end to the Jerusalem revitalization project.[82] Each new tactic increased in severity and potential costs, both to Nehemiah personally and to those choosing to labor with him.

The opposition's first attack was an attempt to discourage Nehemiah and the laborers. The replant pastor cannot underestimate the negative effect of mockery and ridicule.[83] The easiest way to try and stop something is to verbally oppose it. One merely has to spread rumors of what is wrong with the idea and the incompetency of those leading the change, especially imputing shame on those engaged in the work of change. It is basic politics 101. One common tactic used to attack a leader, especially one new to the area, is to question their motive. It prompts doubt without requiring evidence. It is the same tactic used by Satan on Eve in the garden.[84]

The opposition started in on Nehemiah and those rebuilding the wall. Nehemiah's response was to bring their discouraging words before God, asking God to deal with these men opposing the

---

[81] Sanballat became enraged at the news and lashed out at the Jews. Often the godly leader, following Jesus' example, must absorb the anger of the opposition, choosing to respond in kindness and gentleness (2 Ti 2:24-26). (Rabinowitz, *The Book of Nehemiah*, 69).

[82] Nehemiah and those engaged in the work faced antagonism, verbal onslaughts, persistent ridicule and continuing attempts of physical brutality. [Brown, *The Message of Nehemiah*, 1998), 27].

[83] Various Palms lament the painful effect of mockery (PS 42:10; 44:14; 69:20; 80:6; 102:8). [Wijk-Bos, *Ezra, Nehemiah , and Esther,* 1998), 59]. Often community prayer is a powerful response to mockery.

[84] Nehemiah responds by pointing to the glory of God and the integrity of the workers. [Brown, *The Message of Nehemiah*, 1998), 59].

work. He knew as a leader that he needed to stay focused on the task rather than addressing these bogus insults. He would not accept the opposition's low estimate of who he was but rather stood firm by faith in God's calling and God's character.[85] Despite this initial opposition, Nehemiah and the other workers pressed on with the work before them.

The opposition is not put off by their initial lack of success in thwarting Nehemiah,[86] although their anger does grow in its intensity.[87] The replanter must anticipate that those in opposition will adjust their strategy as the replanter counters their initial opposition. They will often meet in secret with certain members of the church in order to thwart the progress of the gospel. The replanter can't be naïve about the opposition. They are often very politically astute and quite skilled in accomplishing their objectives via established organizational procedures.

The replanter has to grasp this given characteristic about passive aggressive people. They do not give in quickly. It is a huge mistake to assume they will just give in and go away because they are quiet. They have tremendous staying power and have outlasted many a pastor in their church. The wise replanter assumes there is more fight left in those opposing the work.

I was once consulting with a church board. During one of the meetings, one long time member was sharing how she had

---

85 Kidner, *Ezra and Nehemiah*, 91.
86 Nehemiah faced deceit and stratagem from his enemies. [Ella Arjenette Rust, *An Exposition on the Book of Nehemiah* (Self Published, 1965), 62].
87 Note the progression of hostility towards Nehemiah. 1) They were annoyed when Nehemiah arrived (2:10), 2) Ridiculed and disparaged Nehemiah when he declared his purpose in coming (2:19), 3) once Nehemiah began making a difference they grew extremely angry. [Rabinowitz, *The Book Of Nehemiah*, 73].

encouraged another member not to leave the church just because that member didn't like the pastor. Her advice was to keep attending, be less involved and wait the current pastor out, for this pastor will move on in a few years. "After all," this leader went on, "It is the New England way." A replanter errs if they assume that the passive people are not strategic in their behavior.

In the wake of initial defeat, Nehemiah's opponents shift to a second strategy. Their new plan was to cause a disturbance and stop the work by force. Nehemiah's first response was the same as before - to pray. He understands that this is God's work and unless the Lord builds the house, the workers labor in vain.[88] Nehemiah needs God's perspective, wisdom, and protection. He knows that he can't ignore the opposition's plans but he begins by first going to God.

After talking with God, Nehemiah realizes he needs to adjust his initial plans. As frustrating as it was, he has to stop the work temporarily in order to protect those engaging in the work.[89] Once their safety has been secured the work begins again in earnest.

However, he could not simply go back to the original plan. Nehemiah has to adjust and develop additional strategies, in light of the current situation. He needed a way to allow the work to continue and yet at the same time protect against this physical threat of the enemy. He continues to adjust the plan as new information becomes available.

---

[88] Psalm 127:1.

[89] Replanting is not about speed but direction and persistence. Often God slows down the replant work because He is doing more work than can be seen, because He has a greater work in mind. Let God direct the work.

For example, one experienced replanter shared how in his first years at the church seven people were actively working to get rid of him. One tactic they used was the children. They unilaterally decided to march the Sunday School kids into the service after Sunday School was over and keep them there in the front two rows so they would be disruptive. When the children were welcomed, these seven then decided to hold Sunday School during the worship service in order to keep the teachers out of the service. Then they changed tactics and threatened to withhold their financial pledges. In each case, they were met with grace but with a gentle refusal to bow to their demands. God, in His timing, frustrated each of their plans.[90]

Also, the replanter has to resist the temptation to discount the tactical information God provides, especially if the information is about someone the replanter thinks can be trusted or is on the inner circle. Stories abound of the damage down by those who appeared to be on the replanter's team but who were secretly plotting his/her demise.

There is also an ongoing wear and tear that people experience with change. The wear is both physical and emotional. Some of it is tiredness and some of it is fear. Often the tiredness amplifies the fears. A fear over whether "this change is the right change," "are those in opposition going to win anyway," "is this really worth all the effort and conflict," and so forth.

---

[90] Mark Devine in his book, *Replant,* talks about those he refers to as the cartel. Four members of his church who over decades had marked out and zealously guarded their turf. "The machinations of these four, in spite of their good intentions, did not result in genuine leadership of the church. Rather, they rendered the church unleadable – certainly unleadable by any pastor anyway." [Mark Devine and Darrin Patrick, Replant, (Colorado Springs, CO: David C Cook, 2014),46-47]

Nehemiah can see it and hear it in the workers. He perceives that there is a need to speak to these defeating emotions. He doesn't let the obvious but unnamed fear gain the upper hand by ignoring it.

The people were afraid of the opposition, so Nehemiah speaks to their fear. He reminds them of who God is and encourages them to be wholehearted in God's work. The solution to their fear was for them to place their trust in God. Nehemiah encourages them, *Our God will fight for us.*[91]

A replant church is typically characterized by spiritual immaturity due to a lack of preaching the historic gospel by previous pastors. There is not a deep understanding of who God is, nor does the congregation have much practice trusting God to honor His word. Thus, there is the need for the replanter to have a patient intentionality in pointing people to Christ from the bible and encouraging them to trust what God has said in His word.

Nehemiah also sets the conflict in a broader context. This work is not just putting them at risk, but it is about the future safety of their wives and children. Their lives were in danger whether they continue the work or not. To move forward was the only viable solution. Nehemiah leveraged their earthly ties and the simple loyalties that are integral to human life to motivate them to be faithful to finish the work God had called them to do.[92]

For many declining historic churches, the only viable solution is to move forward. They are in serious decline and the aging population cannot sustain the church much longer. The church is

---

[91] Nehemiah 4:20.
[92] Kidner, *Ezra and Nehemiah*, 93.

either going to change or die. Revitalization, though difficult and painful for long time members, is the only way forward. The replanter needs to connect this new vision and required change to mission, i.e. to the reality of the church's viability. Often what connects this new vision with the older members is helping them see how these proposed changes would help the church connects with their grandchildren.[93]

It is also important for the replanter to ground the new vision in the history of the church. Unlike a church plant, a replant church has an existing history of how God has used the church in the past. The replanter needs to understand how the gospel was central in the church's past and central to its mission to the community. What is often surprising to these declining theologically compromised churches is that the very thing that they think is the problem, ie the gospel, is in fact the very foundation of their historical success. They replanter can encourage the church to re-embrace the gospel as it is central to them being able to flourish again.

Nehemiah's modified strategy works, and the opposition relents for the time being. However, Nehemiah doesn't think for a moment that they have gone away. Thus, he was repeatedly able to readjust the ongoing plan when new information becomes available.

Another challenge facing Nehemiah is determining which threat is real and which threat can be functionally ignored. One criteria he appears to use is "who is the target of the attack?" When

---

[93] It is not unusual for the dysfunction that is the church to also be in people's families. Often the long term effect of family dysfunction is that the older members are estranged relationally from their children but connected somewhat to their grandchildren.

the attack was against the people as a whole, he took precautionary measures. When the attack was against him personally, he was freer to ignore it. Nehemiah shows remarkable skill in not allowing their shifting threats, ideas, and strategies to unnecessarily impede the work.

Yet, the efforts of the enemy do impede the pace of progress because now half of the men are no longer working but are rather part of the security guard to protect the workers. Nehemiah doesn't allow the reality of the enemy to distract him from continuing on with the work. He makes the necessary adjustments and the work moves forward.

Contrary to Nehemiah's desires, the opposition to the work does not disappear. The earthly source of opposition moves around between various people, but the true source remained the same, for Nehemiah faced a greater spiritual enemy than any earthly opposition. Nehemiah finds Satan engaging in other tactics while the current opposition regroups.

In chapter five, Satan stirs up conflict from within the ranks. The people begin to cry out against the actions of others in the community which are afflicting them. The broken walls of Jerusalem were in part symbolic of the greater problem, a broken community.[94]

We gain a glimpse into the dynamics of working with people as Nehemiah unpacks this problem.

The first dynamic we see about working with people is that Nehemiah takes time to listen and understand what is being said in

---

[94] [Wijk-Bos, *Ezra, Nehemiah , and Esther,* 1998), 62-63].

order to get the facts straight. He doesn't assume he knows even though he has been spending a lot of time with these people. Proverbs warns leaders to not respond before understanding what is going on, "he who gives an answer before he hears, it is folly and shame to him."[95] A key skill required for a leader is the ability to listen and ask questions. Unfortunately, "Words like *teach, preach* and *proclaim* are more commonly connected to ministry than are *listening, reflect* and *ask.*"[96]

Leaders need the facts to lead well, which means that leaders need to do their own investigation. A replanter must repeatedly go through the hard work of getting information firsthand rather than taking the easy route of trusting secondary sources, no matter how trustworthy the sources may be. A replanter can destroy months or years of good will and lose a significant opportunity for ministry by confronting someone about a problem when they have their facts wrong.

A replanter must learn how to dig deeper with people and not take people simply at face value. Simply meeting with someone who is frustrated or irritated to offer moral support is not enough. The replanter needs to ask them what is wrong, why they think it happened, what are their motives and do they have any recommendations.[97] Then those answers need to be substantiated.

I was once on a dysfunctional ministry team that became unworkable. One new member of the elder board took me to lunch and asked me how I was doing but never directly asked me about the

---

[95] Proverbs 18:13.

[96] Steve Ogne and Tim Roehl, *Transformissional Coaching*, (Nashville, TN: B & H Publishing Group, 2008), 123.

[97] "A plan in the heart of a man is like deep water, But a man of understanding draws it out." Proverbs 20:5.

committee. I didn't talk about my understanding of the underlying issues of the team and what I knew to be key contributing causes of the problems, thinking that this was probably a "get to know you" lunch. Imagine my surprise and disappointment when I was told that this person had met with me to get my feedback on that dysfunctional team and had already reported his finding to the elder board, findings that missed key elements of the problem. You can't assume people are sharing their thinking, you need to ask.

Nehemiah hears the details of their complaint. These laborers had chosen to take two months off from their own work in order to devote themselves to the work of rebuilding the wall. This sacrifice of service was exacerbating the already difficult economic hardships their families were facing.[98]

They bring forth the following details surrounding their complaints:

- There was insufficient food for the large number of children.
- Their property had been mortgaged in order to buy food due to famine conditions.
- Money had been borrowed to pay taxes. The result was the alienation of property and the slavery of some of the people. The people had come back from Babylonian

---

[98] Situations are always complicated and the replanter must be careful to not be reductionistic but rather take the time to understand the different nuances surrounding a problem. For example, one factor that played into the economic hardship of those around Jerusalem was the introduction of coinage by Darius around 500 B.C.E. It added yet another middleman into the economic process. There was now another person who also took a percentage of the profits from farmers as the farmers now had to exchange crops for coins. [Blenkinsopp, *Ezra-Nehemiah: A Commentary*, 67].

bondage only to find themselves subject to a Judean bondage.[99]

As a result of this first dynamic of working with people, that of seeking to listen and understand others, Nehemiah uncovers a serious problem of social injustice. Unfortunately, this is not surprising as the issues of social justice are often never far from the community of God's people.

The problems facing the rebuilding effort in Jerusalem were being further exacerbated by social injustice. Nehemiah uncovers that the community was segmented between those who had remained during the exile and those who had recently returned. This segmentation also had economic ramifications since some of the returning exiles seemed to have retained their identity as being economically and socially higher than those who had remained.[100]

Once a community, even a religious community, becomes dysfunctional, it is the poor and needy who usually become the first to be preyed upon in order to privilege the rich and more powerful. This problem is attacked by the Minor Prophets, such as Amos.

The calling of the covenant community is to show the character of God, the one who establishes "justice for the poor."[101] The replanter cannot simple rebuild the religious structures and buildings, but he/she must also address the internal social issues as well. This typically requires confronting the more rich and powerful of the community, often the very ones leading and doing the work. In chapter five, Nehemiah upbraids the nobles and officials, the ones

---

[99] Batten, *The Books of Ezra and Nehemiah*, 238-239.
[100] Blenkinsopp, *Ezra-Nehemiah: A Commentary*, 68-69.
[101] Ps 140:12.

who were addressed in Chapter four as doing and defending the work.[102] It requires faith to confront problems from those who support you and have the economic means to support the renewal efforts. [103]

The second dynamic of working with people that we see from looking at Nehemiah's leadership, is that he understood the powerful influence of spouses. Sometimes spouses speak for themselves as in chapter five verse one, but often they speak through their partner, who is on the board or committee. A team leader must be careful to not dismiss an idea just because it seems out of character for that particular board member to be pressing a certain perspective. If the concern does not make sense then the pastor needs to find out privately why this particular issue is suddenly important to that board member. Often times the pastor will find out that this issue is not that important to the board member but it is to their spouse.[104]

The third dynamic of working with people is, as was mentioned before, the tendency for fatigue to cause people to start worrying and/or to get distracted. When people get tired, they easily lose focus. After the initial stages of the work, the people begin to question the cost and the value of continuing with this vision. The clarity of the vision dims and faith wanes as people get

---

[102] Wijk-Bos, *Ezra, Nehemiah , and Esther,* 1998), 64-65.

[103] Blenkinsopp, *Ezra-Nehemiah: A Commentary,* 68.

[104] Peter Scazzero says it another way, "No matter what kind of ministry you lead, most of the people involved will bring emotional "baggage" from their families. When you are in a meeting with six other people, there are really many other indivisible people present at the table. ... Each of the six people at the meeting come from a family system with certain unspoken rules, values, and ways of doing things." [Peter Scazzero, *The Emotional Healthy Church* (Grand Rapids, MI: Zondervan, 2010), p197].

tired from doing the work. They need encouragement to run the race with endurance.

The fourth dynamic of working with people that we observe from Nehemiah is that when the conflict is internal to the group, it must be addressed. [105] The leader cannot stay unengaged and hope the problem resolves itself. The timing of when to address an issue takes wisdom but rarely is the timing "never." The most common lament the author has heard when interviewing pastors about their tenure as replant pastors was their failure to address an internal conflict in a timely manner, hoping that it would somehow go away or address itself. Yes, it is usually a difficult task, but it is a necessary task of leadership.

Nehemiah gathered the facts and then he takes the initiative to confront the guilty party once he understands the issue. Those in error needed to see that their own actions (some past and some present) were hurting others. It needed to move out of the theoretical realm and into reality. They were hurting real people that they personally knew. Nehemiah implored them to stop and experience the joy of doing what is right.[106]

Often those harming others are quite unaware of it or at least don't understand the depth of the hurt. They need to hear firsthand the perspective of those who have been wounded from those who have actually been wounded. The leader can't be the one

---

[101] Any threat against the unity of the community is extremely dangerous for it strikes at what is typically the church's most precious asset, their unity. [McConville, *Ezra, Nehemiah and Esther*, 1985), 96].

[106] Raymond Brown highlights how Nehemiah arranges his facts to present a persuasive and well-integrated argument. He appeals to conscience, love, morality, theology, scripture, testimony, experience, and commitment. [Brown, *The Message of Nehemiah*, 1998), 90-96].

who shuttles communication back and forth between those offended and the offender(s). A far wiser approach is Matt 18, which may need to be mediated by the replanter, especially in the early stages of renewing a broken church.

Another aspect of this forth dynamic is being willing to listen to reports you don't want to hear. Never underestimate the enemy's ability to use those on your inside circle. It is easy to summarily dismiss reports of disloyalty about those on your staff and thus fail to investigate the truthfulness of these reports. About fifteen percent of those pastor's interviewed reported various levels of opposition by staff. Problems that they were alerted to, but didn't want to believe. As a result, the opposition was allowed to continue and the ultimate damage that was caused was more significant, visible and painful than would have been, had the issues been confronted earlier.

The fifth dynamic of working with people that we gain from Nehemiah's example of leadership is how he helps prevent further conflict by setting a personal example of servant leadership. The life he lived was a shining example of self-sacrifice and hard work. He cared for the people instead of using them to accomplish his own vision. He used his own personal resources to serve those he was leading. Pastors need to be compensated and yet they too need to invest their own resources into the replant church, partly to set a good example.

As soon as Nehemiah addresses the internal conflict, the external opposition is back at it again in chapter six. The opposition hears that the work is progressing along well. They realize time is running out. Thus, they shift their plan from targeting the workers to targeting Nehemiah himself. They try various tactics to remove

Nehemiah. Their goal was to either get Nehemiah completely out of the picture or to at least get Nehemiah to compromise himself so that he lost his effectiveness.

They begin by trying to get Nehemiah to meet with them in private in order to do him harm. The quickest way to stop the rebuilding plan was simply to kill Nehemiah. Leaders are not more important than other laborers but removing a leader is usually disastrous to a rebuilding project. As Jesus said, "You will all fall away because of Me this night, for it is written, 'I WILL STRIKE DOWN THE SHEPHERD, AND THE SHEEP OF THE FLOCK SHALL BE SCATTERED.' [107]

After Nehemiah repeatedly refuses to meet with the opposition, they move to plan "B." Their tactics become creative. They begin to spread lies about his intentions and invoke higher authorities.[108] They send an open letter, contrary to normal civic procedure of that day, thus ensuring that the malicious rumors it contained would sooner or later be public property, further spreading the lies, which they hoped would reach the ears of the king.[109] Nehemiah responds in kind by answering their falsehoods in writing, but he refuses to stop the work. He also keeps praying and asking God for strength.

---

[107] Matthew 26:31

[108] Nehemiah doesn't detail out his suspicions or call into questions their motives; he simply states that he is too busy to meet. Once the work is done he would be glad to meet with them. [Batten *The Books of Ezra and Nehemiah*, 251]. A leader of renewal needs to ask God for wisdom, perception and cunning in order to know what is really going on so as to avoid the arrows of the enemy. [McConville, *Ezra, Nehemiah and Esther*, 1985), 106-108].

[109] Kidner, *Ezra and Nehemiah*, 99. Note, also how the enemy comes across as trying to help by disclosing this malicious gossip and thus attempts to appear friendly hoping to disarm Nehemiah into meeting with them. [Batten, *The Books of Ezra and Nehemiah*, 254].

There is fairly common oppositional perspective in historic New England churches towards a replant pastor that starts to be successful in changing the church. Some of the passive aggressive core members opposed to the replant pastor will continued to attend the church despite not being onboard with the revitalization effort. One reason for this is that historically New England pastors move on after four or five years. Thus, the opposition believes that this troublesome replant pastor is going to give up and leave like all the other pastors before them have done. They simply have to wait him or her out a few more years until things will go back to the way they were.

At some point in time, two things collide as God blesses the work. First, the opposition begins to lose significant influence as the church grows numerically. Second, the opposition realizes the replant pastor is not planning on leaving. Thus, they realize they have to act now or lose the opportunity to stop the change forever. The end result is this: this opposition group will typically put up one last all-out fight to remove the replant pastor.[110]

One typical New England method to remove a pastor is to send out a survey crafted in such a way so as to dreg up any discontent in the congregation about the church and collectively pin it all on the replant pastor. This is then followed by a call for a non-confidence vote in the pastor. As one veteran replant pastor says -

---

[110] The replanter needs to understand the historical strategies used by the opposition in historic churches, as they typically use the same tactics over and over again. In chapters 3 through 5 of *Replant,* Mark Devine gives a great example of how one common strategy of the opposition played out in his church. {Devine & Patrick, *Replant,* 2014), 43-75.

"all a new replant pastor had to do is survive the no confidence vote, but that is typically five to ten years into the replant."[111]

Nehemiah remains clear headed in the midst of these personal attacks. He has resolutely decided that he is not stopping the work regardless of what they say or do. The opposition, undeterred as well, adjusts their plan. They attempt to manipulate Nehemiah by using an insider to distract him from doing the work for so called religious reasons.[112] Their plan was to frighten Nehemiah, get him to make a dumb decision, cause him to sin out of fear, and thus ruin his reputation and the confidence the people have in him.[113] They tried to trick him into hiding inside the temple where he was not allowed to go, since he was not a priest. Nehemiah refuses to yield to fear and stays focused on the work. He once again brings the issue to God and asks God to deal with the insiders. Nehemiah's refusal to accept Shemaiah's warning teaches leaders that they must use careful consideration before accepting advice that appears to run contrary to the work God appears to be doing.[114]

Unfortunately, even after the foundation and the walls have been built, the opposition continues. Opponents continue to monitor the situation via their inside contacts who are still loyal to them, and then they respond accordingly. This is so, despite the fact that the success of the rebuilding work was discouraging to the

---

[111] Dr. William Boylan in private conversation with the author.

[112] Shemaiah was a priest and claimed to be a prophet but was bribed secretly by Sanballat. The replanter must continually pray for wisdom for it is often not clear who is on the side of God and who is on the side of the enemy. [Rust, *An Exposition on the Book of Nehemiah*, 1965), 69].

[113] Our true enemy is subtle. People are merely pawns in the devil's manipulative campaign to frustrate God's work. He masterfully uses the temptation for materialism, hedonism and secularism to his advantage. [Brown, *The Message of Nehemiah*, 110].

[114] Rabinowitz, *The Book of Nehemiah*, 101.

opposition. They understood that the wall was being rebuilt with the help of God, yet it did not deter them from continuing on with the opposition.

Worldly opposition usually understands human dynamics and how to politically advance their agenda. Information is critical to political opposition. In Nehemiah's situation, the opposition was using loyal insiders to gain intelligence. They kept an ongoing private communication stream going back and forth between the loyal insiders and themselves.

These insiders were loyal to the outside opposition primarily due to long term relationships and family. The opposition used these loyal contacts to promote the benefits of their views. They continued to send letters and other communications in an attempt to cause fear and distractions.

In the age of internet, cell phones and the like, it is easy for the opposition and loyal insiders to communicate. The replanter has to assume this communication is happening and continue to teach and speak against the oppositions' reasoning and messaging. Also, the replanter needs to pray and ask God to reveal those plans that will be damaging to the replant.

Nehemiah's response was to turn the people's attention to God. He continually and publically gives God the glory for the work He is doing. He kept reminding the people that this was God's work. It was a work started by faith, and it is faith that will sustain them to finish the work.

One of several differences between the pastor of a local church and Nehemiah is that for the pastor, the opposition is part of the mission field. Thus the pastor must conduct himself or herself in a blameless manner in regard to the opposition so as to be a witness.

As Paul writes:

> *The Lord's bond-servant must not be quarrelsome, but be kind to all, able to teach, patient when wronged, with gentleness correcting those who are in opposition, if perhaps God may grant them repentance leading to the knowledge of the truth, and they may come to their senses and escape from the snare of the devil, having been held captive by him to do his will.*[115]

A pastor must choose to love his/her enemies for the sake of the kingdom and to be an example to the rest of the church. Maintaining cordial relationships with those who oppose you is also good management. The opposition often has a perspective that the replanter needs to hear, even if they disagree with it. Often those outside the inner circle can see and observe things that are difficult to see from the inside. Their recommended solutions may not be on target but their observations may be valid.

I often saw this in the collegiate ministry while I was a student leader. Those who were the oddest in personality and behavior and on the fringes of the ministry often saw the blind spots clearer than those heavily engaged in the ministry. Their recommended solutions were often unhelpful and foolish and thus their observations, which were quite insightful, were also dismissed out of hand.

---

[115] 2 Timothy 2:24-26.

It is helpful to hear what those opposing you are thinking first hand. Personal interaction will help you to treat and think about them as people. These kinds of discussions will help prevent you from boxing your opponents into a particular category (think straw man) and then dismissing them without really understanding them and their thinking, regardless of whether you end up agreeing with them.

The pastor needs to deal with opponents as people. The replanter's example of talking about the opposition with kindness and accuracy will set a good example and help build unity in the congregation despite the opposing ideas.

Nehemiah has accomplished what many considered to be impossible. Its true Nehemiah was the man for the job, but God had prepared him, had worked in people's hearts, engaging them in the work and motivating them to persevere in the work. God had protected Nehemiah, given him wisdom in dealing with the varied strategies of his opponents and giving Nehemiah the stamina to lead this massive work. Plus, God worked in a million other ways that the scriptures don't mention.

Yet, the work was not done. A church replant is often in a far more tenuous position than the replanter realizes. Let's follow Nehemiah as he continues to go deeper with needed changes that will enable Jerusalem to continue to move forward.

CHAPTER 6

LASTING CHANGE REQUIRES INFRASTRUCTURE AND INTENTIONALITY

Church replanting can feel like a false summit. A false summit is when you are climbing and it appears that the peak you are ascending is the top of the mountain. However, the peak you are climbing is actually prohibiting you from seeing the next higher peak. This can happen several times on some mountains.

You think you are almost at the top of the climb, but you are not. You had been encouraging yourself to keep going because you were almost at the top. And then when you get finally there, you realize you are far from the top. It can be deflating. It is easy to begin to question if you can really make it to the top. You have already expended a good bit of energy getting this far and now there is so much more of the climb yet to go.

Church replanting can feel like a mountain climb. You push hard, sometimes over years, to get the replant a foothold. Once you finally get to that first peak, it only reveals the next set of peaks awaiting you. It is easy to become disillusioned that there is still so much more work yet to do. Part of the disappointment is false expectations. Replanters often expect the process to be shorter and easier than it proves to be in reality.

6 – LASTING CHANGE REQUIRES INFRASTRUCTURE AND INTENTIONALITY

At this point in the rebuilding project, Nehemiah has achieved the initial goal of rebuilding the wall. Yet there was still much work to be done in terms of revitalizing the community. We find Nehemiah continuing to model key dynamics of leadership once the initial stages of a replant have been accomplished. He is not under the illusion that the work is done.

A LEADER NEEDS TO BUILD UP THE INFRASTRUCTURE OF THE COMMUNITY.

Once we get to chapter seven of Nehemiah, the wall has been built and the doors have been setup.[116] The community has moved in the direction of health, and some basic key problems have been addressed. Nehemiah now moves his focus to building up the infrastructure of the community.

Nehemiah begins this next round of changes by filling strategic leadership positions with those who are faithful and fear God. He gives his brother and another existing leader a position of trust on account of their character. These two were men of truth, so different from the lying prophets and conspiring nobles.[117]

---

[116] Nehemiah 7:1-6.
[117] Batten, *The Books of Ezra and Nehemiah*, 263.

Nehemiah, after having won so many victories, wants to ensure that all is not squandered through carelessness. It takes ongoing quality leadership to keep revitalization moving forward rather than drifting backwards. His key criteria for choosing quality leaders was to look for those who had already demonstrated trustworthiness.[118]

Leadership development and insightful selection is a never ending part of a pastor's job. It begins at day one. The odds are that the real leaders left the replant church a long time ago. So the replanter is either going to have to develop leaders or recruit them. Either way it takes time.

A common replanter mistake is to wait to build leaders until they are needed. But that is too late. It takes time to build and equip new leaders. The replanter needs to recruit and develop them before they are needed.

Also, a replanter doesn't want to be carrying the burden of a replant church alone any longer than necessary. Pastoring a replant church towards health is a taxing, difficult, often confusing, and a conflict producing enterprise. You can only carry on the battle alone for so long. Solomon wisely said that two are better than one and a cord of three is not easily broken.[119]

In addition, as the church begins to grow, the ministry load quickly outgrows one person, both in terms of the work and the gifting required. The replanter needs additional laborers to do the work, and the church needs leaders with a variety of gifts. Jesus, in Luke 10:2, foresaw this never ending need for laborers and exhorted

---

[118] McConville, *Ezra, Nehemiah and Esther,* 1985), 112.
[119] Ecclesiastes 4:9-12

the disciples to be continually praying for leaders. It needs to be high on the replanter's prayer list.

Also, notice how Nehemiah was particular in who he selected for leadership. He had two critical qualifications: faithfulness and fearing God. Nehemiah only selected those he was sure would be good leaders. Selecting the wrong leaders in the early stages of revitalization can cause delay or serious harm to replant progress.

Another factor is selecting good leaders is understanding the formal process. It is important for the replanter to understand who is a formal member and who is not, especially in congregational forms of government. Critical to safe guarding the progress of a replant is to trim the membership rolls, which typically has never been done. Most historic New England churches have members who haven't attended the church in years. One common New England strategy used by those who don't like the new direction of the church, is to call a church meeting and bring in the old inactive members to vote the pastor out.

James White's belief is that if you ask experienced pastors "what has caused them the most heartache, the most grief, the most pain, and the most discouragement, they'll say, 'People.'" It is not the draining people, those people who require extra care due to weaknesses and neediness, but rather it is those people who are damaging to others.

He shares that his biggest leadership mistake caused his church three years of growth. He hired the wrong guy. The end result was a spirit of division and divisiveness that became a cancer infecting the whole church, leaders, teams, families and individuals. It turned out to be irreparable.[120]

Having no leaders is hard. However, a bad leader is worse than no leader at all. Dr. White identifies five critical things to look for in a volunteer or hire.

1. Character: avoid those with "habitual, pattern & ongoing" flaws.
2. Competence: Ability to get along with others, enthusiasm, positive attitude and raw leadership gifts. Skills can be taught.
3. Catalytic: Create activity, bring energy, have a spring in their step that makes things happen.
4. Chemistry: Do you like them? Would you want to go have coffee with them at the end of the day?
5. Called: would they do this whether they are paid or not? Is this church their home or is it only the job that is keeping them there?[121]

In addition to needing leaders, the physical infrastructure of Jerusalem was sorely lacking. The walls were not the only thing broken. Yet, Nehemiah is careful to not rush things. The community had only begun to reform and needed to learn how to function normally again. He is mindful of the fragility of the community.

For example, only a small number of families actually lived in Jerusalem. This meant that the city was vulnerable to attack when the gates were open unless these few families living there were

---

[120] James Emery White, *What They Didn't Teach You In Seminary* (Grand Rapids, MI: Baker Books, 2011), 69.
[121] White, *What They Didn't Teach You In Seminary*, 2011), 25-29.

completely focused on defending the city. However, life takes time. They couldn't take care of their day to day needs of life and also be focused on defending the city at the same time. There wasn't enough of them.

As a result, Nehemiah does not open the gates early in the morning or leave them open late in the evening so as to accommodate the families living in Jerusalem at this stage. There were not enough men to defend the city when everyone was at home with their families in the evening or when they were tending to the details of life each morning.[122] Plus, it was difficult to find trustworthy men in this treacherous city. Those who lived in the city would have the strongest mctive for fidelity.

Often the church replanter finds a similar predicament. There is only a small number of laborers capable of serving in the church. Thus, their focused service seems so critical to the revitalization of the church. However, normal life starts to get in the way of their service. They have jobs, families, houses that need repair, and so the list goes on and on. The solution, however, is not for people to stop living life but rather to pace the required meetings and ministry around a feasible schedule. It probably won't be the most optimal schedule or the final schedule but the replanter must adopt a church schedule that works for those who are actually serving the church.

The ultimate solution for Nehemiah was to have more families living in Jerusalem. One day in the future it would again be desirable to live in Jerusalem, but it was not at this point. The city was run down. There was still rubble in the streets, most of the

---

[122] Batten, *The Books of Ezra and Nehemiah*, 263.

buildings had not been repaired or maintained for years. Living in Jerusalem meant dealing with extra obstacles. No matter from what angle you looked at it, Nehemiah needed more people living in Jerusalem for this fledging community to be viable. Everything else was a short term fix.

Interestingly though, Nehemiah begins with short term fixes. The longer term solution required additional spiritual foundations to be laid. They needed a deeper understanding of their identity and mission. They needed to know and embrace the truth that they were God's people and that by being God's people they were to value and reflect who God is and what He values. The long term solution had to wait.

Nehemiah took the time to lay the foundation for longer term solutions by having the people taught from the scriptures. He numbered the people by tribe, re-establishing their identity as Israelites. He had the people embrace and commit to living as God's people. These spiritual foundations had to be laid before he felt it wise to initiate asking people to consider sacrificing and moving into the city of Jerusalem. Thus he waited until chapter eleven to begin even having this conversation. Nehemiah knew that people are much more likely to sacrifice and enter into community for the sake of mission and their calling to be God's people.

There is a similar dynamic in a replant situation. The long term solution to many of these problems is more people. In a similar manner, the current environment is often a detriment to more people attending a replant church. The church culture and building are often dated along with the congregation itself. The current style of worship is foreign to the younger generation but well loved by the older congregation. Often the church building is run down, hard to work with, and is difficult to update for ministry in the current decade. All of these can be roadblocks to new members coming and staying at the church.

The replanter needs to make it a priority to meet with any visitors in the following week following their visit. Recruiting new members to a replant is relational and vision oriented. The potential new members is being recruited to you and to what the church is becoming as opposed to the current state of the church.[123]

Retaining visitors is important but the church replanter has to balance missional priorities of his/her calling with the desire of the existing community to maintain the status quo. This is a big challenge. Often, what it takes to attract and retain new members is in direct conflict with the traditions of the existing members who called the replanter to be their pastor.

Often it comes as a surprise to a replanter that the existing congregation actually likes the worship service and has no desire to be rescued from it. The same is true for other areas of their life. Dennis Gill, an experienced replanter, told me of that light bulb moment, when he realized that the people in his declining historic church located in a declining rural area, actual liked where they lived. Since he didn't like the area, he had just assumed that they did not either. The replanter must seek to understand the personal preferences and cultural underpinnings of the congregation.

All the hard work of replanting can be undone quickly if the replanter does not adeptly manage the pace and the amount of

---

[123] This is very similar to church planting,

change.[124] Change is hard and if you push too hard and too fast, the existing members will often dig in their heels and progress will come to a halt. This comes back to the need for a clear understanding of the starting place. Without it, the replanter is apt to misjudge the church's capacity, in terms of timing, resources and infrastructure for various ministry expressions.

Typically, the replanter must be satisfied with short term solutions because the long term solutions require building up and repairing the existing spiritual foundations. The replanter has to take the time to build a vision for outreach. Believers are much more willing to sacrifice for the kingdom and make the needed changes which are contrary to their personal preference, if they understand the missional purpose of the changes. The mission may be clear to the replanter, but it is often unclear to the existing congregation. The replanter needs to give the congregation time to build up the theological categories necessary to understand the details and implications of the vision and mission.

Mission is grounded in identity. The believer is the child of God and a recipient of all that adoption entails. Paul in Ephesians 1 summarizes the present and future blessings enjoyed by the children of God. One responsibility God has given His children is to share the good news of salvation in Christ with others. It is not grounded in duty, but rather evangelism is a response of love for God's grace extended to a sinner. It is one sinner sharing the good news of God's offer of forgiveness in Christ to another sinner.

---

[124] John Kotter at Harvard Business School has identified an eight step model for leading change in an organization: Increase Urgency, Build guiding teams, Get the vision right, Communicate for buy-in, Enable action, Create short-term wins, Don't let up, Make it stick. [John Kotter, *Leading Change* (Cambridge, MA: Harvard Business Review, 1996, 3-7].

The challenge for the replanter is to ground the believer's identity in scripture and within the context of the believer's culture. The temptation is for the evangelical to use the cultural symbols of evangelicalism, which he or she is most familiar with. But in many historic declining theological compromised churches the evangelical symbols are often viewed negatively. The replanter must be aware of the negative baggage these symbols carry.

For example, evangelical terminology, such as the term biblical, is often heard with different negative definitions. Even famous evangelical speakers and writers are not viewed favorable but rather seen as simple minded right wing haters. The replanter needs to vet out terminology and famous evangelical pastors/organizations with trusted members of the congregation to understand what is really being heard by the church attenders. A simple Facebook post or quote in a sermon can greatly damage the replanter's reputation within his or her own church due to such a misunderstanding.

Understanding the import of language is part of the missionary dynamics of church replanting. The replanter must do the hard work of understanding this new culture in which they find themselves ministering. Grasping language is not just making intellectual connections but emotional. People are more likely to change what they do when they are shown a truth that influences their feelings and less likely to change their behavior when they are given analysis that shifts their thinking."[125]

Also, the individual members of the congregation will not all arrive at this understanding of the vision and mission at the same

---

[125] John P. Kotter and Dan S. Cohen, *The Heart of Change* (Cambridge, MA: Harvard Business School Press, 2002), 1.

time. Building a community embraced vision will take time, more time than the typically replanter wants it to take. The replant pastor must recast the vision again and again in a variety of contexts with a variety of methods until God moves among the majority of the people in the congregation. Rick Warren lays out a simple strategy for vision casting in a church in several great articles listed in the footnote. [126]

The replanter will need to describe, explain and promote the new vision publicly. There will also need to be many private conversations with various members of the congregation to answer individual concerns and give them the freedom to express their personal opinions.

These various meetings allow the replanter to gain a growing understanding of several key components that surround the vision. What are the corporate concerns? What are the sub-group concerns? What are the individual concerns? What, if anything, is being misunderstood? Where is there disagreement on future direction of the church? This also should cause the replanter to stay engaged relationally with the subgroups and individuals who may not be supportive of the vision.

Often some of the short term fixes required to keep the replant moving forward are centered on the existing building. It can be difficult to determine how much time, effort and money should be applied to the building and other church resources. Typically, the problem is compounded because the physical structures have not

---

[126]Rick Warren lays out a simple strategy for vision casting in a church in two of blog entries at http://pastors.com/the-4-cs-of-effective-vision-casting/ and http://pastors.com/how-to-share-gods-vision-for-your-church/.

been taken care of due to lack of finances and abilities of an aging congregation.

The good news is that when God begins to grow the church there are often additional funds available. The challenge is determining whether to apply those funds toward new and exciting programs, or forgo those items for less exciting needs such as building repair. Yet, part of stewardship is not being an eyesore to the neighborhood.

The church is not the building and yet the building had a lot to do with both the church's identity and its ability to function as a local church. This remedial work of shoring up the existing physical infrastructure needs to be a priority despite the cost in order to remove roadblocks to people attending and to enable long term sustained growth.

Also, most church replanters have no background in construction, building repair or dealing with historic buildings. Many of these historic churches meet in buildings that have been declared historic buildings. This means there is whole other sets of regulations which must be considered before any changes or repairs can be undertaken. A wise replanter will seek out advice from those knowledgeable in these areas.

Which short term solution is better than another is often determined by the makeup of the congregation. The better the replanter knows the congregation, the more apt the replanter is to recommend wise decisions. Thus, another ongoing task for the replanter is the intentional engagement of the people in the church with the intentional purpose of getting to know each person better and better.

Nehemiah took the time and effort to get to know who the people were, their backgrounds, and their heritage. In addition to helping the people grow in their own identity, Nehemiah realizes he needed to better understand the people, despite having labored together side by side with them for months. God gives him the desire to assemble the various families and enroll them by genealogy. If the nation of Israel was ever to rebuild itself, it was critical for Nehemiah and the people, to understand each family's own personal history.

The replanting pastor may need to remind him or herself that one of pastor's primary tasks is to shepherd the people that God has put in that particular church. The replanter can be tempted to view the existing older congregation as a roadblock to what God could do in that church as opposed to seeing them as sheep in need of a shepherd. IN a similar manner, it is also the fear of the aging congregational members that you won't want to take care of them. You need to both check your own attitude and reassure the older members that you will be there for them.

Shepherding is time consuming work. It will take a significant chunk of the replanter's precious time to really get to know people in the church. It means coming alongside them, at their pace, asking them questions and working on understanding their answers. One helpful strategy is to meet with people in their own homes. This allows the church replanter to gain a better grasp of that family's individual culture.

At one level, this is cross-cultural missions work for the typical evangelical church replanter. The replanter must get outside of his/her culture and enter into the culture of those one is called upon to shepherd. As was stated earlier in the book, understanding the culture of those in the congregation with long term history in the community will pay great dividends in understanding how to reach out to the community with the gospel.

The replanter cannot be satisfied with a superficial understanding of those in his/her care. Each community is different and each has different needs but a foundational part of building up the infrastructure of the local church is simply befriending each one in the congregation.

A Leader Feeds His Congregation on a Steady Diet of God's Word

It should come as no surprise that critical to repairing the spiritual foundations of the community of God is the word of God. One sign that God is at work among the people is an increased desire to hear the word of God. Beginning in chapter eight, Nehemiah, as well as the people, created events for themselves to hear God's word.[127]

The people in and around Jerusalem, both those who had remained during the exile and those who came from Babylon, had not been exposed to the word of God for a long time. As a result, they came face to face with their sin for the first time when they finally heard the word of God. The stark reality of their sin was extremely discouraging.

As the people begin to grasp what God was saying, there was an overwhelming sadness over their failure to measure up to what

---

[127] Nehemiah 8:1-12.

God desired. Nehemiah and Ezra worked at helping them move from focusing on their sin to seeing the salvation of God that was theirs by faith, which was a cause for great rejoicing.[128]

Another means employed by Nehemiah to help people embrace the scriptures was to restore the biblical traditions as we will see in the remaining part of chapter eight. Moving forward successfully is often about timing. Nehemiah was sensitive to respond quickly to what God was doing among the people. Sometimes God's timing requires waiting, other times it means moving ahead of the planned schedule. The church replanter will often feel like the people of Israel in the wilderness did, moving when the cloud moved and staying put when the cloud didn't move.

The people heard the word taught and they wanted to respond. In his wisdom, Nehemiah responded positively and worked to implement their scripturally inspired idea of reinstituting the feasts of booths, though this was probably not in the top ten on his priority list. Nehemiah knew it was foundational for the community of God to understand and respond to the word of God, and this provided a great opportunity. This need for understanding the word of God cannot be taken for granted. The church must embrace a real concern for passing on a knowledge of the Christian faith that goes beyond a meager minimum.[129]

The yearly calendar has long been used by the church to help with the discipleship process. Re-occurring events may not sound exciting but they can be very helpful in reinforcing key concepts.

---

[128] Donald Campbell characterizes the spiritual renewal of Nehemiah 8 as a reverence for scripture, worship of God, comprehension of scripture, remorse for sin, rejoicing in fellowship with God, and obedience to the word of God. [D. K. Campbell, *Nehemiah: Man in Charge* (Wheaton, IL: Victor Books, 1983), 72].
[129] McConville, *Ezra, Nehemiah and Esther,* 1985), 117.

Plus, it takes less work and creativity to repeat an event each year than always creating brand new events and having a certain amount of re-occurring events during the year builds community. Often a replanter can even repurpose existing traditions or attach new ideas to existing values.

For example, the typical historic church has a long history of desiring to serve the community and is sensitive to social justice issues. For most historic churches, the gospel has been stripped from these events, but the desire to serve is still there. Existing service events can be re-architected to include the gospel. The challenge for the replanter is how to tap into this desire to serve but also to re-infuse that service with the gospel.

One replanter recommended that his church hold a thank-you dinner for the town's public works department, which is a critical part of town government. This department rarely gets any public recognition or community thanks for their service. Long term older members jumped onboard to help. Yet, because it was the pastor's idea, he was able to plan the agenda. He was able to merge their passion for service with some brief basic gospel elements in the thank-you presentation. It was a small change but a significant change.

Calendars, events, creative applications, and other infrastructure items are helpful, but you have to keep the main thing, the main thing. A church replanter has nothing of substance to offer people but the gospel. The primary goal of a replanter has to be to re-infuse every aspect of the church with the gospel, from the preaching, to Sunday School, to service events, and everything in between.

Paul, when planting the Corinthian Church was determined to know nothing among the Corinthians except Christ and Him crucified.[130] Paul had a multifaceted approach to preaching Christ, but he was clear that there was nothing else that could save men and women.

The call to pastor is the call to preach and teach the scriptures, both publicly to the congregation and privately among individuals and small groups.[131] Paul told Timothy – *preach the word in season and out of season.*[132] This means that in addition to everything else on the replanter's schedule, he or she needs to continue to grow in his or her preaching skills.

Growing in one's preaching skill needs to be a combination of listening to good preaching and getting feedback on your preaching, both from some folks in the congregation and also from your coach. Yet, these needs must be balanced with the rest of the schedule. You can't spend all week solely on your message. Growth in preaching, like the rest of a replant ministry, will have to be incremental.

In addition, the call to pastor also includes the call to train and develop gifted lay preachers to help carry the preaching load. Most lay people with preaching potential have the time to speak once or twice a year. They will need some initial teaching and coaching, along with regular feedback. Having a bench of two to four lay preachers is a great help to the replanter in carrying some of the preaching load. This further develops lay leaders and gives the

---

[130] 1 Corinthians 2:2.
[131] The apostle Paul set the ministry example of proclaiming the gospel both publicly and privately, Acts 20:20.
[132] 2 Timothy 4:2.

replanter time to address other pressing issues on a regular basis. At one church plant the author was part of, it was our goal for the pastor to only speak three Sundays a month, while the forth Sunday was covered by a laymen.

All of this must continue to be built upon a foundation of prayer. We know from the previous chapters how dependent Nehemiah was upon God throughout the whole revitalization process. Nehemiah was consistently a man of prayer.

This dependency on prayer needs to also be caught by the congregation by adding prayer to corporate events and adding times of prayer to the corporate calendar as fits the local context. The replant pastor needs to pray privately and corporately.

A LEADER IS FAITHFUL TO ADDRESS SIN AS THE COMMUNITY GROWS HEALTHY

By the time one gets to chapter nine of Nehemiah, the community has begun to heal. The progress made by the community allows Nehemiah to begin addressing some specific issues of sin.[133]

Nehemiah provides opportunities for people to humble themselves, confess their sins, and pray. Throughout the rest of chapter nine, this process was accompanied by preaching centered on salvation by faith, and on the hope that they have due to God's lovingkindness, and by employing God through prayer to continue to be gracious to them.

---

[133] Nehemiah 9:1-3.

As we say, Nehemiah understood that when he arrived in Jerusalem not everything could be addressed at once. He kept himself and the community focused on what God had called them to do - build the wall. Everything that did not get in the way of rebuilding the wall was put on hold. Nehemiah was willing to wait until now for God to address problems that did not interfere with this initial basic calling.

Finishing the physical walls provided space for Nehemiah to continue rebuilding the spiritual walls. The central fear of the community over their safety had been addressed, which allowed people to see life and God differently. They now had some basic protection for their families. Addressing that foundational fear had freed up emotional cycles, which created a greater willingness to see and address other issues. One such issue that rose to the surface was the need for the true Israelites to separate themselves from all foreigners.[134]

It is difficult to watch God's people make decisions and do things that make their life and their witness harder. Yet the church replanter has to refrain from trying to fix everyone and everything right away. He or she must emulate Nehemiah's strategic leadership.[135] God will give to the leadership wisdom regarding the timing of when to address sin and foolishness in the congregation as the congregation matures. Often issues of sinful behavior, even by

---

[134] Removal of foreigners should not be viewed as racial exclusivism. As always, foreigners could become part of Israel by conversion (cf. Ezra 6:21; Ruth 1:16–17). [Mervin Breneman, *Ezra, Nehemiah, Esther*, vol. 10, electronic ed., The New American Commentary (Nashville: Broadman & Holman Publishers, 1993), 268.]

[135] Kenneth Hoglund points out that is useful to recognize the Nehemiah's program of reform was first and foremost strategic. [K. G. Hoglund], *Achaemenid Imperial Adminsitration in Syria-Palestine and the Missions of Ezra and Nehemiah, Society of Biblical Literature, Dissertation Series* ed., ed. P. P. David L. Peterson, (Atlanta, GA: Scholars Press, 1992), 243].

those serving in the church, has to wait until the community gains a sufficient understanding of God's holiness and what sin actually is.

One replanter had a key leader living in sexual sin when he arrived but no one saw the behavior as wrong. It took a couple of years of preaching from the bible before a member of the congregation came up to him and asked about whether that behavior was wrong and if so, then maybe that person should not be in leadership. It took more preaching and time until the majority of the congregation came to the same understanding of scripture and the church was able to loving discipline this leader.

The leadership must be willing to confront sin when the community is ready. Issues rarely, if ever, fix themselves. It requires wisdom and patience to know when and how to begin a dialog with people about sin issues. The first step is often overcoming the replanter's and/or leadership's personal fear of shining the light into someone's life. In a similar manner, the surgeon has to get over the fear of cutting someone's skin.

The replanter also has to teach the rest of the leadership how to confront people. A common mistake for replanters is to be the forefront of these confrontations for too long. Once other leaders are capable, let them do the confronting over sin and that allows you as the pastor to be able to come alongside and minister to them.

We know that those who walk in darkness hate to come to the light and often fight the process. However, when sinners do allow God's word to shine in their heart, they find God and experience His salvation over the deeds of darkness.[136] Exposing sin

---

[136] John 3:19-20.

and dealing with the consequences of sin is a hard but ongoing critical component of shepherding God's people.

Part of dealing with sin has to do with rebuilding people's identity as the people of God and re-embracing God's definition of holiness. For Nehemiah, becoming a holy community of God meant separating from the Gentile people around them, both by physically rebuilding the walls of Jerusalem and by religiously reinforcing the Old Testament regulations. The result was a new definition of the community.[137]

Replanters need to stay humble in the process. This means allowing the character failure of former generations to reflect upon his/her own generation. The replanter must be careful to not try to distance ourselves from the local churches' failures of the past out of pride, as if he/she is not made of similar stuff. The replanter needs to accept the sins of this church's past as our own heritage as a sure defense against self-justification.[138]

A Leader Promotes an "Everyone Does Ministry" Culture

Near the end of chapter ten, the community is actively seeking to know and obey God.[139] Nehemiah's next strategy is to start building a culture of "everybody contributes." He lays a biblical foundation of how personal responsibility part of God's call on their

---

[137] Hoglund, *Achaemenid Imperial Adminsitration in Syria-Palestine and the Missions of Ezra and Nehemiah*, 209, 219.

[138] [McConville, *Ezra, Nehemiah and Esther,* 1985), 125-12].

[139] Nehemiah 10:28-39.

lives. God was calling each person to make the building up of His kingdom a priority in their own individual lives.

Nehemiah engages the wider community in the day-to-day work of running Jerusalem by dividing the maintenance work among the people. The tendency of the few to do all the work, while the many stand by and observe, is nothing new.

The starting point in getting the majority engaged in serving (as with most things in a replant) is leadership. Often all it takes, once the community is ready, is simply dividing up the re-occurring maintenance tasks and assigning them to people. Someone doesn't need a special spiritual gift to vacuum the church with their family once a quarter, but odds are the average family won't do it unless it is assigned to them. Besides, serving the community also builds community.

The starting point also includes the existing culture. One's growing understanding of the present culture may require revamping the replanter's own understanding of organizational theory, if the present situation strongly deviates from the previous experience of the replanter. Replanters need reminded that not only are organizations culture bound, but theories about organizations are equally culture bound.[140]

As the Jerusalem community matures, it also began to take on the responsibility for the finances of God's work. A replant is often strapped for finances due to various common reasons. Sometimes it makes sense to enlist outside giving for the initial years

---

[140] Geert Hofstede, *Cultures and Organizations: Software of the Mind* (New York, NY: McGraw-Hill, 1997), 146.

to help get the replant church back on its feet. However, any outside giving needs to be accompanied by two foundational financial pillars.

The first pillar is that those attending the replant need to be supporting the work as best as they can right from the beginning of the replant. Giving needs to be taught and some portion of the budget needs to be met locally, even if the church is receiving significant outside financial help.

The second pillar is that the church needs to be giving to missions in some capacity from the start of the replant, even if the starting amount is small. Foundational to the ongoing success of a replant is that the church is growing in faith and developing an outward focus. Giving to God's kingdom is key component of developing both the church's trust in God as the provider and in building an outward focus.

It is often helpful to tie part of the church's mission giving to other works from the start, as it will engage their hearts in this vision of replanting and encourage them as they replant their own church. This was the author's experience in two church plants he helped lead. Giving to church planting helped the church plant embrace their identity as a church plant and pursue that missional calling wholeheartedly. Bill Boylan, an experienced church replanter from north of Boston, believes that a significant impetuous to revitalization in his church replant was the church's decision to give to missions in the early stages of the replant.

Overtime, most congregations will be able to absorb more and more of the financial cost of the replant work as God blesses. However, that will only be true if the church starts to practice giving. This is a habit that is best started from the beginning of the replant.

This requires teaching the congregation God's principles of giving. It also means creating opportunities for them to give, so they can personally experience God's faithfulness as they begin walking by faith in the area of their finances.

Serving, giving, and worshipping help those in a replant church begin to reorder their week around the priorities of God and His kingdom.[141] It is often a slow process since the world will continue to offer a competing agenda and sinners will continue to be tempting to adopt the world's agenda. It is rarely a straight line to health, but rather an up and down process with the overall trajectory upwards health.

The replanter is always dependent upon God to do what only God can do in the replanter's life and in the life of the congregation. That is to save and change people by faith through the work of the Holy Spirit. Fortunately, those who are part of a church that is becoming a healthy community will begin to encourage each other to run the race with endurance, to lay aside every encumbrance and sin, which so easily entangles us.[142]

Nehemiah also has the congregation begin to honor those gifted saints who step up and take on an even larger share of the work. One side benefit to more people engaging in the work of the church is that this is usually accompanied by a growing recognition of the sacrifice required to do the work. The result is an increased gratitude for those who labor diligently and for those taking on a larger share of the work, including the pastor.

---

[141] Raymond Brown summaries the community of faith's realignment as a promise to pursue God's will, honor His day, value His world, reflect His love, and support His work. [Brown, *The Message of Nehemiah,* 1998), 176-193].
[142] Hebrews 12:1-2.

Besides helping with all the work that needs to be done, there is another reason we want all of God's people engaged in the ministry - gifting. The church needs all the gifts the Holy Spirit has given and thus all the saints are to be equipped and engaged in doing the work of the ministry.[143]

The replanter needs a plan to identify believers' gifting and needs strategies for engaging those gifts in service to the church. There are numerous ministry opportunities in the local church where each gift can be developed and utilized for the good of God's Kingdom. In a healthy church, a high number of ministry tasks are done by those in the congregation, rather than by the pastor and key leaders.

Unfortunately, that is not the culture a church replanter typically finds in a historic church. As was mentioned above, for a variety of reasons, a few are doing some of the work and the remaining few are sitting idle, leaving much of the work undone. Most congregants in historical churches have sat under decades of a ministry model where the pastor does most of what little ministry is done.

This has also led to a mentality among the laity that the pastor works for them. They have hired him/her to do the ministry for them. The biblical concept of call to all the saints needs to be explained and taught in order to break this unbiblical and unhealthy ministry model.[144]

---

[143] Ephesians 4:11-16.

[144] A great book for encouraging people to discern their gifting and engage in ministry is *Courage and Calling: Embracing Your God-Given Potential* by Gordon T. Smith. Also, *Your One Degree*, is a great tool for experienced members to learn how to focus and enjoy God's call on their life. www.youronedegree.com.

This ministry model has left the average person in the pew anemic and underutilized in terms of ministry. As the congregation becomes healthy, the replanter needs to recast for people the New Testament ministry model. This needs to be accompanied by training in how to do ministry, along with the replanter personally recruiting and encouraging people to engage their various skill sets and spiritual gifts in the ministry.

Implementing a ministry model where all the saints are ministering will result in lay people taking on more and more ministry roles. The replanter will need to provide initial training for lay people but ministry proficiency can only be developed via "on the job" training. One implication of this biblical ministry model is that the pastor has to settle sometimes for less than a professional job, especially while lay people learn how to do ministry as they are doing the ministry.

Thus lack of quality, at some level, is the price of developing an "all the saints" do the ministry model. This is a small price to pay for the precious privilege of having additional laborers, despite however painful it can feel in a particularly bad moment of a ministry learning experience.

A second implication of this ministry model is that the pastor cannot micromanage every ministry team and committee. Some highly controlling clergy can demonstrate a certain amount of efficiency within limited boundaries by micromanaging everyone and everything. However, ministry effectiveness will always elude such a style since other people's gifts never get fully developed nor does anyone else develop into a leader.[145]

---

[145] Gange, *Coaching Ministry Teams*, 111.

It is more important that a growing number of people in the congregation engage in the work of the ministry than that everything be done perfectly[146]. The church cannot grow numerically unless those in the congregation are also growing in their love for God and their own skill in doing the ministry which will help support that growth.

The only way people can learn ministry, once they have some basic training, is to personally go about doing various aspects of the ministry. As a result of engaging, they will begin to understand their gifts and what type of ministry grabs their heart. Thus, their effectiveness and joy will increase.

A LEADER TAKES TIME TO CELEBRATE WITH THE BODY WHAT GOD HAS DONE

It has been a long haul for Nehemiah and all those engaged in the Jerusalem rebuilding project. Nehemiah wisely takes time to celebrate with the community what God has done, once the wall is secure and the community is on its way to health.[147]

It was time to rejoice, to dedicate the results of the work to God and to re-consecrate the body to the ongoing work taking place in the city. A great work requires a great celebration. Nehemiah pulled out all the stops in designing a celebration to dedicate the rebuilt wall. He had processionals, choirs, and bands to lead people in a time of great rejoicing.

---

[146] This assumes a basic competency and qualifications.
[147] Nehemiah 12:27-43.

A revitalized church needs to take time to rejoice over what God has done and is doing. It also helps the church body to keep focused on God and not slip into thinking that the ministry depends upon them. It allows people to relax. It takes the focus off all the tasks that still need to be done and redirects it onto people whose lives have or are being touched by God. It reminds the congregation of why it is worth investing one's life in the gospel. It infuses joy in the ministry as people stop to realize and praise God for what He has done, for what He is doing, and for what He will do in the future.

These celebrations ought to happen at various levels in the church. Sometimes they need to be church wide, sometimes within a leadership/ministry team, or sometimes in a small group. The church needs to eventually budget funds for this, so that people feel free to spend resources on celebrating with one another the wonderful God they serve. Some churches build into their yearly schedule a church-wide event for celebrating what God has done in the previous year.

A Leader is Constantly Building and Developing Leaders

Nehemiah took time to celebrate, but he also understood the work was not over. As was stated before, critical to the ongoing work of revitalizing a church is the equipping of each member of the church for a particular work of service. And foundational to the work of equipping the saints is the development of leadership. This principle shows up in the middle of Nehemiah and again near the end of chapter twelve, where there is the ongoing development and appointment of additional leaders.[148]

The same need will be true in the church, for as the congregation grows and as God moves leaders to other places, there will always be the need for additional leadership and staff.

As the church grows, additional functions and needs for ministry are going to emerge, and leaders are going to be needed to oversee these new functions. For Nehemiah, the initial need in Jerusalem was protection and guarding what little they had. Once Jerusalem is restored, the needs shift from guarding to providing. Batten points out that in Nehemiah 12:44, the role of the men appointed over the storerooms was not to guard the stuff collected, but rather to see that a good amount was kept on hand.[149]

Where will these leaders come from? The wise church replanter develops a plan to address this future leadership issue at the start of the replant. The replanter must wholeheartedly embrace that part of his/her job description is the ongoing recruiting and equipping of leaders.

The process starts with understanding what a biblical leader looks like from God's perspective. Nehemiah was clear about what were the kind of people he wanted as leaders. He wanted leaders who understood the importance of intentional leadership, teamwork, hard work, and adherence to scriptural guidelines. The church replanter needs a clear understanding of these qualifications prior to recruiting someone to leadership and prior to investing significant time in developing a particular individual. Sometimes God

---

[148] Nehemiah 12:44-47.
[149] Batten, *The Books of Ezra and Nehemiah*, 284.

provides leaders to the congregation who are already prepared, but the majority will need to be developed from within the congregation.

Early on, additional leaders may also need to be recruited from other sources to assist the church replanter in leading and shepherding God's people, if the church has limited numbers. Trained leaders can be recruited among those with parachurch backgrounds, and also among other churches interested in supporting church replanting efforts, plus local seminaries and bible schools.[150]

In many New England church replants of the past 40 years, the difference between forward progress and stalling was the replanter's ability to re-insert the role of the pastor into the leadership selection process. The specifics for appointing lay people to various ministry and committee leadership positions will vary by denomination. However, the qualifications, selection, and development of leaders are critical decisions, of which the church replanter must be a part.

This task of recruiting and equipping is always ongoing because there is always a need for future leaders, and occasionally God moves existing leaders elsewhere. Additional leaders will always be needed if the ministry is to grow beyond the capacity of the church replanter. There will be a growing need for elders, deacons, small group leaders, and other ministry positions in a church replant, especially as the church becomes healthy. The

---

[150] Overseed is developing a network of regional New England Overseed Hub churches who are tithing some of their resources, both financial and human, to help resource church replants in their early stages of renewal.

church replanter cannot wait until the church is healthy to begin this process of developing leaders.

Another reason you cannot wait to get started is because it takes too long to build leaders. The time to begin developing leaders is always now. Existing members need to be assessed for leadership potential, and those with leadership gifts will need to be equipped. It takes precious time to build leaders but it is time well spent. *Leaders who divest themselves of power and invest in others will find that the initial investment has grown.*[151]

A LEADER IS ALWAYS UNDER THE WORD OF GOD

Nehemiah is a man of vision and accomplishment. He was a "can do" kind of guy. Yet he was clear that the work of God has to be done according to the will of God. One cannot go about ministry as one likes, but only as God desires. There are biblical standards regarding how one is to behave in the ministry, how the ministry is to be done, and the kind of ministry that God desires.

The people of Israel began to adopt this same mentality of Nehemiah. They began to want to do life and ministry God's way. As one gets to the end of Nehemiah's account in Chapter thirteen,[152] the people of Israel are making ministry adjustments themselves as they sit listening to the word of God.

---

[151] Ford, *Transforming Leadership*, 199.
[152] Nehemiah 13:1-3.

It was an encouraging time in Nehemiah's ministry and yet the work was not done. So too for the replanter, there is still much more gospel work to be done (and there always is).

Rebuilding walls is easier than rebuilding people. We know that people don't want to come to the light lest their sins be exposed.[153] Even though the promise of forgiveness and healing is always held out to us by God, we need others to help us face our sin, confess it and repent. Sometimes that help needs to be applied corporately, but usually it needs to be private.

Being under the word of God requires the replanting pastor to speak the truth in love to those in church, which often exposes sin either in thinking or in action. The temptation for the replanter is to leave out certain parts of the truth which are uncomfortable so he or she doesn't have to have difficult conversations with people. The replanter must not allow him or herself to avoid taking the initiative to interact with people over their sin.

Yet, the truth must be spoken in love, both in what is said and in how it is said. The content must be the truth, but it has to be wrapped up in grace. Whether speaking to the church corporately or to individuals, there must be a sensitivity to what the congregation understands graciousness to be. For the replanter, who spends much of his or her ministry talking, this means taking the time and effort to carefully make good word choices, to adopt gracious tones of speaking, and to adopt appropriate body language. The replanter must do what it takes to lovingly communicate truth to both the church culture and the community culture in which he or she is ministering.

---

[153] John 3:19-21

The replanter must research and think through how his or her language and manner of speaking is being heard, yet at the same time being careful not to transform or change the content of the message while contextualizing it for his or her congregation. For God and God alone dictates the content of message.

One issue that a replanter often faces is the issue of syncretism. Ezra and Nehemiah are faced with the same problem as Joshua upon entering Canaan, how to deal with a foreign people and an unbiblical culture. Merging the Jewish faith with the religions around them was not a biblical option. The absolute condition required by God for fulfilling His promises to the Israelites was separation and sanctification. Nehemiah and Ezra were motivated by religious convictions which required a religious verdict. [154]

Syncretism must be addressed over time. When a church has not been under biblical preaching, over time it will adopt the thinking of the culture around them, yet while often maintaining biblical language. The world quickly begins to squeeze the church into its mold of thinking, often through this redefinition of biblical and religious terminology.[155]

This can also take the shape of alternative forms of worship and prayers, accepting behavior that is sinful, and teaching ideas that are unbiblical. The replanter must graciously and patiently move the church back under the authority of the scriptures.

The responsibility to be under God's word also extends to the entire church leadership team. God encourages leaders to be

---

[154] S. Japhet, *From the Rivers of Babylon to the Highlands of Judah* (Winona Lake, IN: Eisenbrauns, 2006), 113.
[155] Romans 12:1

creative, ask questions, and pursue ideas. Yet there are boundaries. Leaders cannot merely use people in attempting to accomplish their goals. Leaders cannot manipulate others into doing what they want. Leaders cannot neglect their own spiritual habits.

The replanter's life needs to permeate humility as a servant of God. This is the mindset that we see in Philippians three, where Paul describes his great personal achievements as rubbish. Replanters cannot fall into the trap of somehow thinking that they are the most important person in their church, that they deserve to be treated with deference, and that greater allowances ought to be made for their weaknesses and so forth.

The replanter is just a fellow follower of God seeking to use his gifts to God's glory. When people start making excuses for your behavior and manner of speaking, something is wrong. They ought not to be making excuses for the replanter but rather admonishing him/her to repent (if needed) and mature in Christ

Being under the authority of the scriptures also provides clarity to the goal and purpose of ministry. The ministry is about the gospel and encouraging people to trust God's message to them. There are many offshoots of ministry that spring from there, but the foundation of the church is the gospel message of Christ and Him crucified. The replanting pastor will spend his or her entire ministry unpacking for people what faith in the gospel means for both justification and sanctification.

The word of God is the standard to which the church and the church replanter are held accountable. The replanter will help his congregation and help himself stay close to the will of God by constantly putting the word of God in front of the church and by seeking to personally apply that word.[156]

We have seen how Nehemiah continued to lead the revitalization of Jerusalem after the initial goal of rebuilding the wall had been accomplished. Nehemiah had achieved some basic stability, and the city of Jerusalem was established and functioning.

However, there was more work to be done. Nehemiah took on the additional work of appointing additional leaders, upgrading the city infrastructure, implementing a division of labor, ongoing vision casting, dealing with specific sin issues, stopping to celebrate, and continuing the process of developing a new generation of leaders.

Nehemiah knew that he had to be intentional about developing the infrastructure of Jerusalem if there was going to be any lasting change. At this point in Nehemiah's career, he and the people had made significant progress implementing and upgrading the infrastructure of Jerusalem and yet Nehemiah knew the job wasn't complete. And yet, there was still more work to do.

The replanter must be careful to not declare the replant a success too soon. The end goal is not a fragile replant but a healthy flourishing church. Until the church reaches that point, there is still a defense posture that must be maintained to protect the replant from attack or self-imploding.

---

[156] 1 Timothy 4:16.

CHAPTER 7
REVITALIZATION IS AN ONGOING PROCESS

Author: When does a church plant become just a church?

Church Plant Guru: Good question, at some point it does.

The same is true of a replant. At some point the replant church needs to lose the distinction that this is a church in renewal and it needs to move on to being a church. It needs to embrace its full identity as a church and all of what it means to be a church of Jesus Christ.

7 – REVITALIZATION IS AN ONGOING PROCESS

Revitalization is hard work and leaders are tempted as time progresses to want the process to be done, for the goal to have been reached. On one hand it is true, just as a church plant at some point ceases to be a plant and is just a church, so also a replant at some point ceases to be a replant and is just a church. Yet, all churches have to continue to move forward or they begin to digress. When they digress they need renewed. Second Timothy 3:16 depicts this ongoing process of renewal, both for individual and churches.

On the other hand, just as the work of personal sanctification is never finished this side of heaven, so corporate sanctification is never complete either. Nehemiah continues to always find out that there is still yet more work to be done.

By chapter thirteen, one would have expected those opposed to Nehemiah and his rebuilding project would have admitted defeat and would have gone away. Unfortunately for Nehemiah, the opposition does not disappear.[157] As time goes on, the reader finds that the opposition's goals and desires were more complex and diverse than was apparent at the start.

Nehemiah's opposition waits for yet another opportunity to try to regain a footing in the organization. Often, the way in for outsiders is via a family member or through an existing relationship with someone who is an insider. Nehemiah had to return to the

---

[157] Nehemiah 13:4-31.

King[158] and his absence was the opportunity for which Tobiah had been waiting.

Tobiah was related to Eliashib, the priest, who had responsibility for the chambers of the house of our God. Eliashib had a large room used to store grain offerings, frankincense, utensils and other tithes. He had this room cleaned out, prepared and gave it to Tobiah as a personal residence. This kind of action was clearly prohibited by the scriptures and you would think a priest would know better. However, Satan is very adept at using relationships to leverage allegiances in order to tempt people to do his will because so often people value the approval of others over the approval of God.

Upon his return Nehemiah is extremely displeased with this evil that had been done by Eliashib. Nehemiah dwelt with this problem swiftly and fully. He threw Tobiah's household goods out of the room, had the room cleansed and had the utensils along with the offering and frankincense restored.

The cycle of renewal and then decline often repeats quicker than anyone expects. In chapter thirteen, the people wane in their enthusiasm and start to neglect their spiritual duties. Ongoing faithfulness takes intentional work; coasting is easier but it quickly leads to drifting.

The church in every generation must fight against allowing the world to squeeze it into its mold, (Rom 12:2). Israel's problems here fell into three categories (a) failure to maintain the purity of

---

[158] It is important that the leader keep his word and obligations to those outside the organization. Nehemiah had made a commitment to the king to only be gone so long and when the time was up he was faithful to return. [Batten, *The Books of Ezra and Nehemiah*, 290].

religion and sanctity of the temple, (b) desecration of the Sabbath and (c) intermarriage with foreign women. These are all interconnected, because foreign influence is present in each.[159] Syncretism is active at many levels of thinking and motivation.

Nehemiah couldn't assume that he knew what was going on from a managerial distance. He had to be personally engaged in the work. There is the temptation for the replanter to disengage from the work once the revitalization has taken root under the pretense that they did all the hard work up front and now it is time for other people to carry the load. Yes, other people need to be laboring, but that is not an excuse for the replanter to disengage from doing the work himself or herself.

As Nehemiah worked alongside others in the community he discovered that some new problems had developed. Some of the community leaders over the time period that Nehemiah had been gone, were no longer being faithful to carrying out their duties. They were not running the race with endurance, but rather they were dropping out. Like these leaders it is easy to drift, to make exceptions for yourself as a leader, and to cut corners as time goes on.

Nehemiah knew that what happens in the life of leaders quickly replicates itself in the life of the followers. This unfaithfulness couldn't be left unaddressed. He reproves these leaders for their dereliction of duty and for their unfaithfulness to God.

We also see an underlying truth at work in this rebuilding effort at Jerusalem. On the positive side, various factors and

---

[159] McConville, *Ezra, Nehemiah and Esther,* 1985), 146-147.

strategies are working towards renewal. However simultaneously on the negative side, factors and strategies are working against renewal. One set may be more obvious than the other set, but both are always present and the replant pastor must be aware that both sets of dynamics are at work in renewal. We would like to think that the enemy has been defeated and left the premises, but the evil one is still at work.

Nehemiah also addresses this area of leadership again. He determined that additional leadership was required to shore up some particular areas of weakness. Yes, you need to give people time to grow as leaders. However, at the same time you also need to keep the key areas of leadership staffed with capable people. Sometimes this means moving leaders to different areas while they develop, and sometimes it means removing a leader who is not gifted. Obviously timing and process is critical, especially in the early stages of a replant.

Ongoing revitalization requires that the shepherds continue to work at being aware of the state of the individuals in the congregation. When the inevitable problems are discovered, they need to be addressed with wisdom, and humility and according to church and denominational procedures. As a pastor, the replanter must embrace the reality of ministering to sinners. It should not be surprising that sinners will keep on sinning, nor is there any need to be frustrated at the mess which must be cleaned up.

A godly leader must never give up or shrink back from the responsibilities of the calling because sometimes things get messy. William Carey suffered innumerable hardships as a missionary. He attributed his success to plodding. In his later years, he shared this with his nephew, "I can plod. That is my only genius. I can persevere in any definite pursuit. To this I owe everything.[160]

This ongoing work of knowing and understanding the congregation extends to the replanter knowing him or herself. Don't forget that as a replant pastor you come with your own baggage, just as Nehemiah did. Growing in self-awareness is an ongoing need.

A key area of self-awareness for a replant pastor is his/her own emotional health. Unfortunately, for most replanters the art of managing their own emotional health was never part of their discipleship or ministry education. Thus, this area requires greater attention and diligence or it will leave the replant pastor vulnerable and often incapable of dealing with problems in a godly way.[161]

Another problem uncovered by Nehemiah was that the Israelites were neglecting the importance of the Lord's Day. Neglecting the Sabbath was harmful to the community. Those returning from the exile should have been keenly aware of this, especially the leaders.[162]

Nehemiah again begins with the leadership, pointing them back to the word of God as the standard for living. Once Nehemiah had the leadership on board, he was able to implement practical solutions to address the problem.

In like fashion, the replanter needs to begin the implementation of any change by addressing it with the leadership

---

[160] S. P. Carey, *William Carey* (London, England: Hodder and Stoughton, 1923), 23.
[161] For more information; Peter Scazzero, *The Emotionally Healthy Church* (Grand Rapids, MI: Zondervan, 2010).
[162] In 2 Chronicles 36:20-21, the author grounds the primary cause for the Babylon exile in Sabbath breaking.

first over the word of God. Pastors need to work at not surprising their leadership but not including them in key decisions. Surprises often demotivate other leaders and engenders resistance, even to changes they might have otherwise embraced.

The problem of neglecting the Lord's Day is not just an Old Testament problem. The average family today has many conflicts on Sunday morning. The shepherd needs to know the state of their flock and what people are doing on Sunday. We are not under the old covenant law, but Paul did warn those in the church not to neglect gathering together on the Lord's Day.[163]

Once congregants have gotten out of the habit of attending church regularly on Sunday, the solution to helping them get regularly involved again typically requires the initiative of the pastor or lay leader. Part of leadership and discipling of others is helping to facilitate progress. Families may need help thinking through how to manage their families in a society where Sunday is no longer guarded for them. Creative ideas can go a long way in helping the community build good habits.

Nehemiah also set up a means to keep himself informed of this particular problematic situation until he was convinced real change had occurred. The replanter will find that as the church grows he/she is going to no longer be able to be involved in everything. The church will have additional leaders and information flow will need to be more intentional and institutionalized. The replanter pastor will need to set up feedback loops in order to stay informed about important ministry initiatives and their progress.

---

[163] Hebrews 10:25.

The replanter may find that other leaders react to this process of setting up new procedures, as these can easily feel like the resurgence of bureaucracy. This can provoke deep emotional reactions from long timers, since typically part of the reason for the church's decline in the first place was stifling bureaucracy. However, because bad systems were in place previously does not mean that good systems should not be implemented. All growing communities need increased infrastructure. The challenge is implementing positive infrastructure only when it is needed.

Another reason to minister alongside of people is this allows the replanter to stay personally involved with the congregation so he or she can truly "one another" those in the congregation. Nehemiah's experience shows us that one area which often requires regular diligence is helping people take sin seriously. In order to do that it requires knowing people well enough to be able to come alongside them in order to help them see and repent of sin.

Nehemiah was not disengaged or aloof from the people God called him to lead. He was observant and concerned about them. Again it was when Nehemiah was among the people that he was able to observe that something was seriously wrong. The Israelites were intermarrying with the local Gentiles. And again, Nehemiah had the courage to address the problem despite the very difficult implications. He could have easily left the problem for the next governor to deal with but instead he chose to personally deal with the problem.

The problem required extremely difficult discussions and heart wrenching decisions. Nehemiah had to be bold in dealing with this sin that was beginning to permeate the community and because it was also endangering the community by provoking the wrath of God.

While the text doesn't comment on Nehemiah's methods, it appears to the reader that his deep desire for the welfare of Israel's community is being funneled through anger. Certainly he should have been angry at the sin, but he appears quite angry in the midst of applying discipline. It may be contextually that this was required and maybe this is appropriate in a government position but definitely not in the ministry. In the ministry, anger can be an effective tool in producing behaviorism, but it does not work in producing godliness.

The long term wear and tear on Nehemiah must have been significant. He is approaching the end of his tenure, and he doesn't want all this work going to waste. It may be that this is what fueled his frustration and anger.[164] For the replanter, weekly diligence is required to manage his or her own emotional health. Otherwise, there is the significant danger that the replanter will get desperate and respond in anger or become disengaged and respond by disengaging. Protecting against this emotional unraveling is particularly important as the ministry continues over the years.

Dr. Bill Boylan is beginning his forty-seventh year in ministry at the church God called him to replant. He believes that the key to his ability to maintain emotional health was being personally clear that his call was not to fix people but to love them. He was to love them regardless of the problems they caused and issues that spun up around them.

---

[164] The text doesn't tell us so this is only speculation on the author's part.

Ministry that is effective to people requires that the leadership be continually engaged with the people, so that at least one of the leaders know each individual attendees personally and how that person is really doing. When needs are uncovered, the leader needs to work to provide what is needed, When sin is discovered, the leader must take the difficult steps to confront that person about their sin, calling them to repentance and forgiveness. If this person happens to also be involved in leadership, then the disciplinary process may require removing them from leadership for some time period as Nehemiah had to do.

Speaking of Nehemiah, Charles Spurgeon wrote, "We are not called to govern, as he did, with an iron hand, but we ought to be equally inflexible, decided, and resolute for God, and for His holy will." In other words, God calls us to *Be Determined!* [165]

Lasting change requires a replanter to be diligent about knowing the ongoing state of the flock, to not tire of the constant need to re-teach, re-organize and shore up areas of weakness. The replanter must also always remember that this side of the second coming, we are not eliminating sin and its influence. The evil one is always lurking beneath looking for an opportunity to resurface and regain a foothold, thus the replanter must be diligent to continue with the work God.

A replant pastor at some point turns into being a pastor, but the work of shepherding, leading, worshipping and evangelizing are never done. Being a church replanter is a wild ride that will test one's faith, one's management acumen, and above all one's ability to love sinners. However, only the pastor gets a front row seat in

---

[165] Warren Wiersbe, *Be Determined* (Wheaton, Victor Books, 1992), preface.

watching God do an amazing work in the life of a church and the lives of the individuals of that church. Being a pastor is a privileged calling! Keep at the work. May you be able to say confidently with Paul:

> I have fought the good fight, I have finished the race, I have kept the faith. Henceforth there is laid up for me the crown of righteousness, which the Lord, the righteous judge, will award to me on that Day, and not only to me but also to all who have loved his appearing. [166]

---

[166] 2 Timothy 4:7–8.

CONCLUSION

If you plant a church in a larger city you can die your hair red, wear whatever you want, and put out a shingle for new church plant. Nobody is challenging "why are you here?" because they think you do not belong here. No, you and this new church are just another facet of living in a diverse city within a transient population.

However, if you move to a town 20 miles from any city in New England, you stick out like a sore thumb, and it is obvious "you are from away!" as they say in Maine. There is a huge question mark on your head, and it can take numerous years to begin to gain trust from the locals.

Yet, if you come to the same town as the new pastor for the downtown historic church than from the local's perspective "you are supposed to be there." You fit a familiar context and it is easier to build the bridges of relationship. Replanting a historic New England church is a missional strategy to reach a community for Christ from the inside out.

CONCLUSION

The more I have studied church replanting, the more I am convinced that this is a key evangelistic strategy for New England. Unlike church planting, church replanting starts from a historic trajectory within an existing congregation.

Replanting means bringing gospel change to an existing congregation. This change begins with the replanter. Once a church is broken and in serious decline, often the only way forward is to hire a replant pastor who will pray for them, who will once again preach the historic gospel, and who will lovingly lead the church.

Nehemiah models for us how to lead change in the midst of difficulty and opposition, how to start with what is and move it forward to health. The city of Jerusalem was broken. It was broken physically, spiritually, and civically. Yet, by the end of Nehemiah's tenure the city had significantly healed. Physically, the wall was rebuilt and the gates were restored. Civically, the city's infrastructure had been restored. Spiritually, the people were once again worshipping God.

As we have walked along with Nehemiah and watched as he led the Israelites through this amazing transformation, we have learned a number of lessons on leading revitalization that apply to the church replanter. Yes, the context is different between a civic leader and a pastor. Yet there is also much overlap and many of these leadership lessons learned from the life of Nehemiah are helpful to the church replanter.

LEADING A CHURCH REPLANTING/REVITALIZATION PROCESS MEANS:

- *BEING CALLED OF GOD.*

  1. A leader must care.
  2. A leader must pray and be willing to wait on God's timing.

- *RESPONDING TO GOD'S CALL*

  3. A leader must plan.
  4. A leader understands the importance of position.

- *BEGINNING THE REVITALIZATION PROJECT*

  5. A leader understands that the ministry takes a tremendous amount of organization, planning, timing, and communicating.

- *PUSHBACK*

  6. A leader must expect and respond to continued opposition to the work of God.

- *LAYING THE FOUNDATION FOR REVITALIZING THE COMMUNITY*

  7. A leader needs to build up the infrastructure of the community.
  8. A leader feeds his congregation on a steady diet of the word of God.
  9. A leader is faithful to address sin as the community grows healthy.
  10. A leader promotes an "everyone does ministry" culture.

11. A leader takes time to celebrate with the body what God has done.
12. A leader is constantly building and developing leaders.
13. A leader is always under the word of God.

- *REVITALIZATION IS AN ONGOING PROCESS*

14. A leader is diligent about knowing the state of the flock and does not tire of the constant need to re-teach, re-organize, and shore up areas of weakness.

This writer's focus has been on the particulars of leading a church replant/revitalization in a historic, declining, often theologically comprised, New England church context. There are many overlaps to other types of church ministries but need for New England replanters is now.

The book began by describing how leading a historic New England church replant is no easy task. It is even harder in a historic mainline church for those unaccustomed to its culture. Replanting a church has some similarities to becoming a missionary in a different culture. Replanting is a difficult work but also a highly rewarding work as one is able to minister with God on the front lines of a community.

Nehemiah was able to accomplish much in a short time frame, yet the work of revitalizing Jerusalem was a long-term task. It extended over the remaining years of Nehemiah's life. The call to replant/revitalize a church in order to reach a community for Christ is also a long term calling, often for life.[167] It takes many years to rebuild the foundations, train leaders, and lead the church towards health. Deciding to take a pulpit in a historic church for the purposes of replanting cannot be seen as a stepping stone to a better position. Rather it is a decision to invest your life in a particular location among a particular people in order to share the gospel with them.

The call by God to replant/revitalize a church is a significant and wonderful calling. It is also a call to be a good leader. Nehemiah has given us a broad example of the skill sets needed and of the kinds of circumstance the church replanter is likely to face in a replanting/revitalization work.

Nehemiah had honed many of those skill sets while working for government and faithfully carrying out his civic duties to the King. God began to move once He had prepared Nehemiah and the people of Jerusalem for this revitalization project. The life of Nehemiah is an important example of how God can use a leader who is submitted to God and who desires to live, not for their own glory, but for God's glory alone.

It is my prayer that God is raising up numerous church replanters who He will send out in the harvest. There are thousands of churches across America and particularly in New England, which are deeply in need of revitalization.

---

[167] *25 to Life* is an initiative to support and encourage long-term ministry in northern New England that seeks to foster the spiritual growth required to embrace and overcome the specific cultural challenges of pastorates in this cold and stony land of New England.

My prayer is that God is calling you or has already called you to replant one of these historic churches in order to awaken their surrounding community to Christ.

TOP 10 CHARACTERISTICS OF A CHURCH REPLANTER

1. **Sacrificial Calling** [not just a ministry opportunity] **to a particular church with particular issues, embracing state/local culture and the history of the local church.**
2. **Good marriage, spousal cooperation, healthy ego strength**
3. **Comfortable with conflict, willing to live in the tension of a theologically compromised environment, ongoing discernment of what is essential/non-essential, a grace giver, nonjudgmental, committed to staying in the denomination** [Doesn't need to be surrounded by theological purists]. **Can live in tension of the call to be both a chaplain to surviving few and church planter to the community.**
4. **Gospel Centric, perseveres because of belief in the power of the gospel, clearly & proficiently proclaims the gospel, and waits patiently for the Holy Spirit to cause the seed to sprout.** [Not a quick fix or methods orientation, able to live in the grey without speaking grey]
5. **Relational about the gospel ministry, loving, thick skinned, listens, human solidarity as a fellow sinner** (Doesn't take everything personally, works through conflict, builds bridges of relationships in a distrusting environment, classic pastoral/shepherding skills, adjusts to their culture)
6. **Reaches the lost** (in the church [including those who think they believe] and the community, able to think missiological about the church), **vision to replant this church as a means to reach this community and then to replant other churches and reach other communities for Christ.**
7. **Recruits and develop leaders** [not passive]

8. **Unapologetic about leading change, nurtures and leads change within the context of the local church authority structures, into and through the inevitable crisis moments** (Starts with what they have and builds from there, not a blast and rebuild mentality)
9. **Builds community and teams, embracing and respecting who is there** (among the old timers, new comers, older and younger generation)
10. **Teachable and coachable** (history of mentors/coaches, able to find & be sustained by encouragement outside church, not a lone ranger)

APPENDIX B – STAGES OF DECLINE

Quick Replant Church Assessment Tool

Church History

❑ (1) --------	❑ (2)----------	❑ (3)---------	❑ (4)---------	❑ (5)-------
Long Decline Conflict	Declining Conflictual	Living In The Past	History Straight-Jacketing Vision	Building On History

Culture

❑ (1) --------	❑ (2)----------	❑ (3)---------	❑ (4)---------	❑ (5)-------
Distrusting Ingrown Dysfunctional	Change Slow Vision Conflict Apathetic Submerged Tension	Traditional Institutional Resistant Few Lack of Unity Visitors Isolated	Blended, Hopeful Tiring over dealing with problems Some Reaching out	Thankful Engaging Worship Living as a family Seeking to live out Vision

Leadership

❑ (1) --------	❑ (2)----------	❑ (3)---------	❑ (4)---------	❑ (5)-------
Abdicated Matriarchal / Patriarchal	Power Struggles People won't serve Moral failure	Competing Visions Opposition working behind the scenes Members vs Pastor	Good but silo'd Leadership Wrestling with vision Leader/Staff conflict	Working at staying unified Moving vision forward Staff/Leader levels consistent

Structures

❑ (1) --------	❑ (2)----------	❑ (3)---------	❑ (4)---------	❑ (5)-------
Disorganized In Disrepair No Money	Income can't meet basic expenses Mismanaged	Basic structures in place Income meeting basic expenses	Struggling with vision vs income	Using structures as a means to accomplish vision

Congregation

❑ (1) --------	❑ (2)----------	❑ (3)---------	❑ (4)---------	❑ (5)-------
Mostly NonChristian Hurt/Angry Engaged, Older <30 people	Divided Spiritual Dry <50 people	Generational mix Allusion of Safety Some embarrassed by church <80 people	Struggling with vision vs income <140 people	Using structures as a means to accomplish vision

Ministry

❑ (1) --------	❑ (2)----------	❑ (3)---------	❑ (4)---------	❑ (5)-------
Sunday service No pastoral care	Sunday service Some CE Some Pastoral care Community events	Sunday service Basic youth group Some small groups and discipleship	Sunday service CE, Youth group Small groups Some vision inspired ministry	Ministries aligned to vision Functioning as a local church

Missions

❑ (1) --------	❑ (2)----------	❑ (3)---------	❑ (4)---------	❑ (5)-------
None	Little giving Social justice but little gospel	Seen as extra but some supported	Becoming outward focused Concern for community	Becoming missional

Theology

❑ (1) --------	❑ (2)----------	❑ (3)---------	❑ (4)---------	❑ (5)-------
Bible is irrelevant	Biblically illiterate Sin is affirmed	No overarching theology or concern about it	Wrestling with gospel and its implications for life and ministry	Moving gospel into practice

Total Score: _____

RESULTS INDICATE:

Based on the total score above, use the chart below to identify the stage of this church.

Score	8-12	13-20	21-28	29-36	37-40
Stage	4	3	2	1	Healthy
Description from Nehemiah	Wall Broken Down	½ the Walls are there	No Gates	Need People	Growing Community
Word Picture	Sinking	Damaged, taking on water	Adrift	Moving Slowly	Functioning
Time to Reverse Stage	1-4 years	1-4 years	1-4 years	1-4 years	Ongoing

Stages of Church Decline

Key Identifiers	- Stage 4 - Walls Broken Down	- Stage 3 - 1/2 Walls There	- Stage 2 - No Gates	- Stage 1 - Need People	- Healthy Church - Growing Community
History	Long decline, conflict	Declining, conflictual	Living in the past	History straightjacketing vision	Building ongoing history
Culture	Distrusting, ingrown, dysfunctional	Change slow, vision conflict, apathetic, submerged tension, new comers isolated	Traditional/institutional, resistant few, lack of unity	Blended, tiring over dealing with problems & reaching out, still hopeful	Seeking to live out vision, live as a family, thankful, engaging worship
Leadership	Abdicated, matriarchal/patriarchal	Power struggles, people won't serve, moral failure, members vs pastors	Competing visions, good vs bad leaders/staff, opposition working behind scenes	Good leaders but silos, wrestling with vision, staff & leadership levels consistent	Striving to stay unified, working at adjusting/moving vision forward
Structures	Disorganized, disrepair	Income can't meet basic expenses, mismanaged	Basic structures in place, Income meets basic expenses	Struggling with income vs vision	Using structure as a means to accomplish vision
Congregation	Mostly non-Christian, hurt/angry, unengaged, older, <30 people	Divided, spiritually dry, <50 people	Generation mix, allusion of safety, some embarrassed by church, <80 people	Some spiritual growth and engagement in ministry, some inviting others to church, <140 people	Growing maturing, desire to serve
Ministry	Sunday, no pastoral Care	Sunday, some CE & pastoral care, community events	Sunday service, basic youth group, some small groups and discipleship	Sunday service, CE, youth group, small groups, some vision inspired ministry	Aligning ministries to vision, functioning as a local church
Missions	None	Light giving, social justice but little gospel	Extra, but some supported	Becoming outward focused, concern for community	Becoming missional
Theology	Bible irrelevant	Biblically illiterate, sin ok	No overarching theology or concern about it	Wrestling with being outward focused, having concern for community & world	Moving gospel into practice
Word Picture	Sinking	Damaged, taking on water	Adrift	Moving Slowly	Functioning
Typical Time to Reverse Stage	1-4 years	1-4 years	1-4 years	1-4 years	Ongoing

WHY OVERSEED

Hope for the Historic New England Church

New England (NE), according to a recent Gallup poll, is the least churched area of the US, while probably having the most churches. These declining historic churches, like the typical New England lawn after winter, need overseeding, in this case with gospel seed.

Most historic New England churches have been declining for years, suffering from problems whose root stems back to the pastor veering away from the historic gospel message. The result is typically a declining, non-gospel centered, church.

Typical New England

The result is two distinct but related problems: churches which no longer function like the church and a history of pastors who are not preaching the historic gospel message.

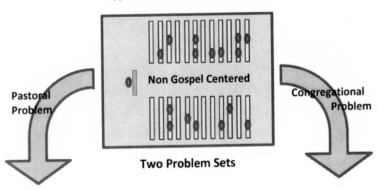

Typical New England Church

Non Gospel Centered

Pastoral Problem

Congregational Problem

Two Problem Sets

The Way Forward

Overseed believes the way forward begins with prayer and intentionally embracing renewal strategies that address these two problem sets.

1) Overseed recruits pastors and students to serve in these churches, who are committed to the gospel message. Overseed provides coaching for those called to pastor within this unique environment of a renewal church setting.

Overseed's three year coaching curriculum is designed to prepare pastors for the practical dynamics of a pastorate in a renewal context. Coaching helps equip pastors to plant themselves in a historic church / community for the long haul.

2) Overseed engages declining historic New England
    churches about pursuing a path of renewal. Overseed
    coaches local church leaders in how to guide renewal
    efforts based on the historic gospel within the context of
    the story of their church.

Overseed also partners with larger regional churches who
can provide pulpit supply, coaching and other resources in order to
help declining churches in surrounding communities.

Overseed addresses these problems as follows:

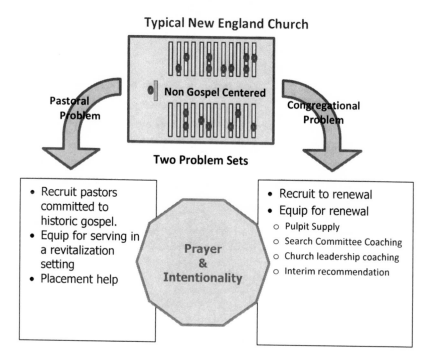

Typical New England Church

Non Gospel Centered

Pastoral Problem

Congregational Problem

Two Problem Sets

- Recruit pastors committed to historic gospel.
- Equip for serving in a revitalization setting
- Placement help

Prayer & Intentionality

- Recruit to renewal
- Equip for renewal
  o Pulpit Supply
  o Search Committee Coaching
  o Church leadership coaching
  o Interim recommendation

The Larger Picture

Overseed helps to connect churches needing pastors with potential candidates who are committed to the historic gospel and have been coached in leading renewal in a historic New England church.

Renewal is typically not a quick endeavor and can be especially draining on young pastors and their wives. Besides hosting various conferences, Overseed works with various networks in New England such as the Barnabas Group, 25 to Life and eNet Roundtables, which are all designed to support pastors and encourages them to enable long term pastorates, which is critical to renewal.

Overseed also works with denominational leaders in identifying opportunities and renewal strategies fitting the particular context of New England and each local region.

Overseed recruits on various seminary campuses, bible schools, and among collegiate para-church groups by sharing this vision of replanting New England churches and offering coaching to those students who are interested.

Vision

Overseed's vision is to replant/revitalize declining historic New England churches in order to awaken communities to Christ:
- By recruiting & coaching historic church leaders in intentional renewal strategies.
- By recruiting & coaching pastors to serve in these churches.

Strategy

Overseed focuses on these declining historic New England churches because they are one of the key missional methods for reaching New England communities for Christ. They already have a building and resources, plus relational and historic connections to their community. Besides being missional, this strategy mirrors the heart of God, who delights to renew His church, both by giving His people a desire to know Him deeper and by giving them a leader who will help them.

Overseed's intentional revitalization strategies include: strengthening what is foundational; remodeling existing ministries; fixing what might be broken; & building new ministries.

Team

Overseed's president and co-founder Jim Harrell earned his Doctorate in Renewal from Gordon Conwell Theological Seminary. Overseed's board of directors consists of experienced regional New England church leaders.

Overseed's team seeks to serve local churches and pastors by:

- Providing seasoned pastoral coaches to coach pastors in a renewal church setting.
- Providing experienced church coaches to coach leaders in guiding renewal efforts.
- Partnering with larger regional churches who aid other churches in their renewal efforts.

Overseed's mission is all about helping historic New England churches grow deep and reach out.

For more information about Overseed church replanting network, go to www.overseed.org/about.

ABOUT THE AUTHOR

 Dr. Jim Harrell is president and co-founder of Overseed. He has his Doctor of Ministry in renewal ministries and Masters of Divinity from Gordon-Conwell Theological Seminary. Jim's background is discipleship, mentoring and church planting/replanting.

Jim came to Christ in the Christian Missionary Alliance church where he grew up in Vermont. He was student leader with The Navigators at college and helped start the work at the University of Miami and also ministered at the University of TN. After that, God called him out of The Navigators to minister in the local church. He helped with two church plants in Burlington, VT, where he was the unofficial associate pastor of the second church plant.

Jim moved to the Boston area in 1999 to finish seminary and began attending Byfield Parish Church, (a UCC denominational church), which is where he caught the vision of replanting churches in existing historic congregations. Jim applied his background in church planting, shepherding and training towards developing a plan for this replanting vision. The outcome of that process was the formation of Overseed, Inc.

It is Jim's passion to help declining churches to thrive once again by re-embracing the gospel and by moving out into the community with the message and service of Christ.

CPSIA information can be obtained at www.ICGtesting.com
Printed in the USA
BVOW07s1819100315

391094BV00003B/34/P